SOLITARY GOOSE

SYDNEY LANDON PLUM

For those who formed the circle—

Terry, Trevor, and Hilary Plum,

Donna Evan, Phoebe Lehmann, and Connie Warren—

and for animal rescuers everywhere.

Lone wild goose, not drinking, not feeding,

flies crying, calls out his longing for the flock.

Who pities his lonely form,

lost from the others in ten-thousand-layered clouds?

I gaze to the end of gazing, still seem to see him;

so great my sorrow, I seem to hear him again,

while crows in the field, wholly unconcerned,

go on as before with their raucous cawing.

Du Fu, "Lone Wild Goose"

Contents

Acknowledgments

I want to extend special thanks to the people who have been supportive of this project and my writing all along. Thank you to Ann Zwinger, Terry Tempest Williams, and John Elder. Thank you to those good listeners Rachel Stein, Allison Wallace, Suzanne Ross, Lorraine Anderson, Susan Hanson, and Bernard Quetchenbach. I appreciate the opportunities provided by the Association for the Study of Literature and Environment and the Bread Loaf Writers' Conference.

Thank you to my friends and colleagues at the University of Connecticut, Storrs, who have also been very supportive: Jean O'Reilly, Joan Joffe Hall, Lynn Bloom, Susanne Davis, Jerry Phillips, Sam Pickering, and John Manning in particular. Thank you, Tom Jambeck, for listening to stories about geese at lunch.

I owe an enormous debt to John Tallmadge, whose editorial skills shaped this book and sharpened every page. The staff at the University of Georgia Press is terrific, and I am especially grateful to have worked with acquisitions editor Judy Purdy. Thank you to the editors of *Interdisciplinary Studies in Literature and Environment* for publishing a version of "Two Geese and a Duck on a Pond in Winter" and for allowing us to include a version here.

There are not words enough to thank the wonderful people at the Kensington Bird and Animal Hospital and the Hungerford

Outdoor Education Center, as well as all the special people who are wildlife rehabilitators. You deserve more recognition.

My parents, Barbara and Ned Landon, encouraged me to play outside. They have also read and listened to excerpts from this book with patience. My children, Trevor and Hilary, not only figure in these exploits, they (along with their spouses, Brandy and Michael) also have had to read great portions of the manuscript. They all have been kind and generous throughout. For the will to persevere I thank my husband, Terry Plum, who never doubted me—and that made all the difference.

Years ago, as I wrote down the first notes about a goose I called SG, I made a promise to him and to a collie named Charity, who spirited me around the pond daily. I promised I would tell this story. I have kept that promise, because I always had them in my mind and heart, if no longer in my life.

SOLITARY GOOSE

Two Solitary Figures

During the late fall and early winter of 1996–97, I made daily visits to a pond near my home where there was a solitary Canada goose. During the darkest part of the winter, I went to the window in the dining room at night and pressed my forehead against the glass, which was quite cool and slightly damp. With my head against the glass, I talked to "sg," the solitary goose. I had been talking to him for months—about the weather, the conditions of life on the pond, about my life and my dog's—but my winter's-night monologues were on a different note. At night I asked him to be careful, because of the coyotes and foxes; to be strong, against the wind and cold; and to be brave, against loneliness and despair. I stood in the dining room, late at night (sometimes in the middle of the night) and asked a solitary goose to be careful, strong, and brave. Sometimes I asked him to be patient. Just wait for me to get there in the morning. Stay alive until morning. Now, looking back at this time, seeing myself—head resting against a window, seeming to look out into darkness—I realize how appropriately this image embodies my involvement with the solitary goose. Facing a window at night, in a lighted room, I would have seen only my own reflection.

It was not until much later that I realized I had to take into account the reflection in the glass in order to write about a landscape with two solitary figures—held separate in their different spheres by experience and language—and about the darkened glass that constantly throws one figure's reflection back, rather than letting her see clearly what is in the world.

Across the road from the house, behind the school, is an entrance to a wooded preserve maintained by the town. Schoolhouse Brook Park is part of a much larger land trust that extends throughout the town. The trust encompasses several local preserves of southern New England mixed deciduous forest and wetlands. As the park and the larger trust are on lands reclaimed from the small farms and orchards that replaced the original forests, there are stone walls and foundations, old mills and the evidence of mill wheels, remnants of orchards, and other signs of past human use. And there is fairly heavy contemporary human use. Walkers, bikers, runners, hunters, boaters, fishermen, swimmers, picnickers, birders, naturalists, scientists from the university, teenage lovers, and underage drinkers frequent the woods and waters.

Bicentennial Pond was created by the damming of Schoolhouse Brook. To get to the pond from my home on Spring Hill Road, I crossed the road, skirted the school's tennis courts and soccer field, and then entered a little margin of woods on a path. About seventy feet farther, the path opens onto a half-acre picnic area, just at the crest of a slight incline. Down the grassy slope of the incline is a brief, man-made beach. Then the pond spreads out its nearly six acres. It is both a dammed and dug pond, fed by natural springs and a brook; there was a smaller body of water before the current pond was created in 1975, a year before the anniversary for which it was named. During the time of my acquaintance with the pond, the depth of the water and its quality were monitored. One might hope that this was out of concern for the ecology of the area, but primarily it was because the pond was the town swimming hole from late May until mid-August.

The pond is stocked for fishing in the spring, and for two or three months after the beginning of fishing season there are people at scattered sites around the pond every morning, some of them seeming to have camped there. Paths, maintained by the town and a group of volunteers, score the woods. In the late fall when the trees are leafless, you can see all the paths at once. The landscape appears flattened, like a painting without perspective. One path goes most of the way around the edge of the pond, so that, walking it, you can almost always see where you have been, where you joined the circle.

A booklet describing the trust and this park offers a self-guided nature tour and is sold in the town hall. The posted regulations that restrict usage of the pond and park, the aerator and drainage system in the pond, the existence of a booklet describing a nature walk established nearly thirty years ago—all these represent the imprint of New Englanders' "steady habits" on the land.

In spite of the intensive human use, the pond and adjoining woods have an integral place in the lives of scores of birds and animals who move in and out of the immediate environs, depending upon the season of the year and the time of day. Deer materialize all year at dusk and dawn, leaving their footprints in the soft earth and their scat in slightly dispersed piles. Raccoons, possums, and skunks leave their prints, most noticeably in the snow and in the soft mud at the edge of the pond. Sometimes in the winter there is print evidence of the trail that the fox takes along the margins of the woods and fields and the frozen pond. Sometimes the coyote leaves scat on rocks in the middle of the trails. We are more often aware of coyote presence listening to their singing in the night.

Hawks nest in the woods near the pond: red-tailed hawks are common, but once a goshawk hung around for a few weeks. He flew so low over me that I could see the mottling of his breast feathers, feel the disturbance of his wings. I think he was checking me out as a food source. A juvenile osprey used to make a brief visit in the spring and fall, and I saw him dive into the pond and emerge, shimmering in the sun like molten metal spraying un-forged droplets—with a stocked trout in his talons.

In the spring and fall, a kingfisher sometimes sits on the hand-rail provided for swimmers with disabilities. A pair of ducks returns to the pond late in February, followed by the Canada geese. The geese and ducks are present in even larger numbers in September and October, when they congregate before their win-ter movements. The crows and woodpeckers and songbirds of a mixed woods provide the soundtrack for the woods according to their season. Killdeer skitter and cry along the edge of the pond from late spring until early fall. Kingbirds sail above the pond in the early mornings of May and June catching bugs and reflecting light from their silvered breasts.

In describing the pond and its inhabitants, I want to set the scene and let you know what ordinary is. This is what can exist on a pond where humans make their noise and leave their scent and waste: food, cigarette butts, plastic and Styrofoam containers, aluminum cans, fishing lures and lines. Schoolhouse Brook *is* a park: it has been shaped by human means to accommodate hu-man use that is both formed and informed by taking place where the forces of nature have not been completely overwhelmed. It is a bit of earth shared nearly equally by human and nonhuman life. All the evidence is there to show how natural systems work, with the advantage that there are also opportunities to observe how natural systems work their way around human disruption.

I walked the trails in the woods year-round. I had begun by wanting to identify everything, from the Frost's bolete (a fungus that looks like upholstery velvet) to the seven different kinds of acorns I had separated into the wells of an egg carton. However, identification is rather like a full stop on the walk, and I wanted to keep going, stay on the trails. I began to work on knowing where the Frost's bolete would come up, and through what kind of leaves, after what weather, at what time of year. I wasn't really a part of any of the systems, but perhaps I could at some point help to keep things steady.

In September the Canada geese begin to make their large, intricate, aerial patterns, drawing attention to themselves with their nasal cacophony. There are few things as reassuring in the world as the cyclic behavior of migrating wildlife. There are few things that are a greater source of melancholy. The migration of birds powerfully stirs our hearts, brings a response from our imaginations: coming back and going away. It represents constancy, yet it is composed of multitudinous, individual changes—and goes on in its stream without us. The migration of birds reminds us that we rarely feel that our individual, short-spanned lives are a part of something so sensible, ordained, and generational. On a September morning you can stand in the middle of an expanse of grass and hear the Canada geese honking and feel as if you might belong to the universe the geese inhabit. However, most of us feel irreparably cut off from the unity of nature. Is this a function of culture or of biology, of our nature? Must we always stand outside nature because of our knowledge of our own mortality? Watching the geese year after year, I know that this experience is not the same, that I am not the same, as last year or the year before. One day the geese will fly over the grass and I will not be standing there.

Geese float on the pond fairly constantly from late summer until a large portion of the pond freezes over, usually in mid- to late November. Reflected on the surface of the pond, on a sharply focused autumn day, the Canada geese seem to me majestic. Would others agree with this aesthetic judgment? Perhaps the way we perceive the physical world—the emotions, inspirations, intelligences arising out of looking around—is not really so arbitrary. How we see is at least in part a product of physics. The sharpness of the image in the New England autumn is in its own way as pleasing as the softness of the landscape of northern Italy, so often remarked upon by painters and poets. Perhaps you cannot credit the effect of specific, localized habits of lighting until you experience them. Even having read Ruskin and Keats, I was unprepared for the effect of early morning light on the hillsides of Umbria. The physics of these sorts of visual impression are examined in *The Nature of Light and Colour in the Open Air*, by Marcel Gil Minnaert.[1] He suggests several explanations for the phenomenon of the sharp, clear, brilliantly colored reflection—in this case of Canada geese on this small pond in autumn. The sun is at a lower angle with every passing day. The angle of the light upon the water changes both the intensity of the reflection and the "interference," which is light bounced back up from the depths. As fall progresses, there is less humidity in the air. There is a difference in the quality of the reflection given by water blown away from the sun, as compared with water blown toward the sun.

In late September, I might see fifty or more geese resting in the clear light with their images reflected below them, the grays and blacks and whites forming an abstract of colored patches against the blue of the water, which is also a reflection, of the sky and the greens and browns of the surrounding landscape. Carelessly, the viewer drifts into an aesthetic vision influenced by emotions. Deciduous trees, appearing gloriously lit from within at this time of year, frame the pond for more than half its circumference. In every season I am afforded a different version of the pond, from the flowering of the swamp azaleas, which seems to mirror the evening light, to the brazen autumn colors, visual antiphony to a light fading into winter. In winter, one pale aspen at the water's edge near the middle of the eastern shore relieves the starkness of the woods, and the pond.

There are strong emotions within us, ready to be stirred by something out there. In the autumn I am under the spell of the Canada geese: whose sensuous forms swim and glide and rest upon the sharply faceted water; whose reflections form an abstract pattern of color where the water and the sky are one; whose migrations symbolize continuity and community, in flight above me.

Looking back to the fall of 1996, I see that I had been if not preparing for the encounter with the goose, at least training for it. Several years before I had been at a writers' conference, working on an essay noting the parallels between the dry season New England was experiencing and my own personal state of emotional and intellectual aridity. I knew that I wanted the traditional Pueblo story of Yellow Woman to somehow shape the story I was telling. Yellow Woman is one of four sisters representing both the cardinal directions and the colors of the types of native corn: yellow, white, red, and blue-black. I am one of four sisters, a fact that has shaped my life in ways I have never been able to articulate. In some versions of the story, when Yellow Woman is kidnapped by a demon-lover (or runs away with him, depending on the version of the story and its cultural and curative intent), her sisters call her back. They sing to her, and she—living in the mountains far in space and, given the nature of the story, in time—hears them and returns to the village. The natural rhythm is restored: the rains come, the corn grows, babies are born and nurtured.[2]

I was very lonely in the autumn of 1996. I struggled with the various aspects of my life that isolated me, even from friends and family. Having withdrawn from marginalized academics, I had neither the social identity nor the sense of community that work provides. The editorial work I did was solitary; its product generally obscure. I was not financially independent any longer, which offended my Puritan roots and my '60s feminism. All around me I saw women doing what I did not seem to be able to do: maintaining the sense of self necessary for a career, while still managing the constant small immolations of nuclear family life. All of this weighed upon me in my solitude. I was hoping to be called back to something I would recognize as "the right place"—where I would be connected and creative.

I had the leisure to structure my own days, and I went to the pond with the dog often, sometimes taking notes. Whatever I deemed noteworthy at the pond was usually the result of some connection I tried to make with a bird.

25 September 1996

Lowering the water level of Bicentennial Pond seems to have increased the bird activity around the pond. This morning when Charity and I arrived, 45 min. later than usual, there were a dozen Canada geese honking at us from the water, and killdeer skimming the surface of the water. The light caught the pale buff underside of a flying killdeer and my eyes followed this beacon to the far part of the pond, where the inlet neck widens, where a heron stood fully stretched out in the sun. I walked slowly down the hillside and he didn't stir. From there, about 60–75 yards away, I walked slowly toward him: taking 5 or 6 careful steps at a time and pausing for quite a while between movements. I had to trust there was nothing to trip me, for I dared not take my eyes off him. And I fought off the distractions of the wandering dog, the darting killdeer, the honking geese, the squirrels squawking in the trees and sending nuts thudding down. I learned my lesson from the disappearing blue jay that if you take your eyes away from a bird for even a second—he will be gone.

The heron remained remarkably still, even when the dog came up level with me briefly (I was not doing anything interesting, so she went off again). He would change the angle of his head periodically, but did not seem afraid or ready to fly off. It did not seem to me that he ever looked right at me. When I got to the edge of the pond on one side of the small inlet within which the heron perched on a rock, I was 20–30 feet away. I thought I would squat in the grass and watch to see if he would go after the fish jumping just 15 feet in front of him. As I squatted down he gathered himself together and flew to the other side of the pond, which was not far away but was in the shade so that I could not see him as well, his dusky gray camouflaged against the mudflats exposed by the lowered water level. He composed himself with his neck settled into an S curve so that he was more compact.

I felt that if I moved away, he might feel comfortable about going back to his original, sunny perch, so I turned and set off through the muck uncovered on my side of the pond. But the heron stayed put.

Looking down I saw the vegetation now exposed to the cool autumn morning. Starlike clusters of thick, spongy grass blades formed a pattern across the mud reminiscent of a kimono design. Here and there were lily pad fronds, wet and flattened against the pond grass.

My eye caught on the pale iridescence of an opened mussel shell, then I noticed them everywhere in the muddy area. Someone had been having a banquet on stranded freshwater mussels.

Walking down into the really mucky area, where I sank an inch or two with each step and had to pull my feet out to move, I saw many more brown, closed-up, still-living mussels. For twenty minutes I sucked my way through this mud, prying up mussels and plopping them back into the water. Some were 4, nearly 5, inches long and had the heft of the mottled rocks they resembled. They made a satisfying sound as they hit the water, and even the heaviest of them floated briefly before slipping into the water and settling to the bottom.

The geese had stopped honking, though the dog was still nearby and I was throwing things into the water. While I saved mussels two more small groups of geese arrived, and though they honked their arrivals and their noisy, wing-flapping, feet-splashing landings, as soon as they were on the pond they took their cue from the original inhabitants and quieted down.

When I got to the end of the beach area, which was also the end of the grass and the stranded mussels, I looked back to the heron, who was still scrunched down on the shady side of the pond.

The lesson from the blue jay was learned on a walk while at the writers' conference—a walk on which I had several remarkable experiences, several visitations. The last of these was by a blue jay who insisted on having attention paid to him. He flew into a branch just above and in front of me as I walked along Route 125, vocalizing that unprovoked blue-jay rebuke. I noted his presence, but kept walking. He flew out from behind me and landed in front. Insistent. We leapfrogged down the road until I stopped and looked up at him. "Hullo. What do you want?" He chastised on for a bit. I was looking right at him. Then his voice seemed to come from somewhere else, and I turned my head in response. When I turned my head back, after what seemed like merely a fraction of a second, he was gone. I hadn't heard him fly away, and blue jays are usually noisy in flight. I couldn't see him in flight or landing in any of the nearby trees. Was the blue jay a warning? A promise? A mirage? After that experience I was much more careful to keep my eye on things. Even things that seemed to *want* to be noticed can simply vanish.

My first note of a "lone goose" in my journals is an offhand comment among recordings of the heron's continued presence and of the last full lunar eclipse visible from North America in the twentieth century. The goose was on the pond in early September. He would paddle around alone, or accompanying the pair of mallards who were revisiting their spring haunt. When the flocks of geese descended, he was absorbed into their numbers.

I delighted in this constant animal presence at the pond. I talked to him, from the beginning of our acquaintance calling him "sg" for "Solitary Goose." Behind this naming lay all the Romantic burden of the solitary: from Jean-Jacques Rousseau's "Solitary Walker"[3] to Wordsworth and Byron, Jane Eyre on the moor, Audubon and the figures of the American West. By reflection I romanticized my own solitary presence at the pond.

We were two solitary figures. I started talking to him as soon as I came over the hill; talked to him walking toward the pond; stood on the beach and talked to him. After a while, I noticed he seemed to swim around the pond paralleling my walks. I kept filling up the peacefulness of the woods and the still pocket of air above the pond with my chatter—a habit that I scorn in others. I was sure that one morning I would come over the hill calling out "sg" and he would be gone. Yet it did not happen. September went by, and most of October, and scores of geese had come to the pond and gone on. A few still came, but less often. I had been assuming that SG had simply gotten separated from his flock and that at some point he would join another. Geese mate for life, but aside from that pairing their communities are loosely knit. In fact, juvenile geese are strongly "encouraged" to drift away from their parents, undoubtedly through some biological realization of optimum breeding possibilities. SG seemed slight enough to be a juvenile; he just needed a new group of guys to hang with. But he stayed on the pond: the only eremitic Canada goose on record. In SG, the solitary goose, I found an occurrence in the natural world that seemed to mirror my loneliness, thus lifting the burden of unnaturalness I felt.

I clung to this delusion, this distorted view of SG's life and situation through the dark glass of my unhappiness, in spite of the mounting evidence that something else was at work in the natural world, the world outside myself. There we were: two solitary figures. Each in our own landscape. Our respective spheres had common elements: the pond and the curve of trees around it demarking the cup of sky above, the night and day; the rain dimpling the surface water of the pond and beating down the grass and rushes along its bank; the sun making the pond a reflection of the world we saw. Isolated within my imperfect vision, the solipsism of my internalized response to the world I saw and walked through every day kept me alone—even on this, our common ground.

I wonder how many others have wandered into the natural world and put pen to paper out of a sense of loneliness. Cast out or cast down, our impulse is to turn a face to the sun, the clouds, the rain. The perfected world, the world as it was made, calls to us in our moments of isolation, when we have let go of everyday thoughts and voices grabbing us into the fray, the babble. Enjoying in solitude the perfection that we see in the natural world is terrifically healing. In this world we see, animals are mirrors that we use to return back to us an image of ourselves; they are unmarred by our frailties and our knowledge of death. Animals are also our companions, when the solitary healing is not enough, and we look for companions to guide us to wholeness, or to give benediction to our loneliness and the errors that caused it. Even if, like Rousseau, we are solitary because we perceive that the rest of human society has failed, solitude rarely brings delight—although it may bring wisdom. In his self-exile, Rousseau had a gamekeeper import a pair of rabbits to a lonely island to create a little nexus of activity and life for him to admire, only to discover that this was not wisdom, but an action rooted in melancholy.

Whatever healing may occur is likely based upon a misunderstanding of the physical world. We put ourselves into the world of animals and plants, of rivers and trees and the mountains and the carved-out bottom of the ocean—as if we could just slip back in. As if understanding could give us a place in the web. Mostly nature does not need us; it goes on without us, separate from us. How can mere intellect bridge that separation? Furthermore, given the separateness of, for instance, animal lives, how can we say anything about them that is not simply the back of our own minds, cast upon a silvered surface? What is the exit from this hall of mirrors? How do we *know* anything of the natural world? Perhaps I was refusing to acknowledge the actual plight of the solitary goose because to do so would mean giving up the solace I felt in viewing a landscape with a solitary goose in it, the promise I read into my version of the landscape.

I began to feed the geese as a way to get to know them, to get to know SG. I did not want SG to be eating out of my hand; I wanted to know him as an animal, *as his own presence*. If this response was part Jody in *The Yearling*, it was also part Alice. I needed something to be curious about. In the years that I had been visiting the pond, I had not really committed myself to making the visit a daily habit. Like having farm animals, the feeding of the geese began to seep into the fabric of my existence, closing up little interstices of time, and pulling the whole into straighter alignment with the schedule of the sun and the subtle shiftings of the light.

In the early days of feeding the geese, I sometimes allowed my different obligations to keep me from the pond in the morning, and I often walked over at noon or in the early afternoon. Rarely was there anyone to be seen at these times: not a goose to be found on the pond, trying to graze on the increasingly barren hillside, or nibbling at the last few kernels of yesterday's grain pile. Thus, I continued to believe that the solitary goose flew off during the day, and only returned in the evening—alone, or with a "borrowed" flock with which, for some reason, he did not choose to stay when they moved on.

One November morning I was feeding the geese and, as usual, sg had been one of the first to trundle out of the water and bobble in that almost elegant way up to the grain, only a few feet away from me. All of the geese had gotten used to me, had even grown to an uneasy tolerance of the dog—as long as she did not move suddenly as a predator might. I had come to know sg not only because he was often the first in front of me (the first in line for food), but also because I had come to realize that geese are recognizable as individuals. The lengths of their necks vary, as does the shape of the white chinstrap each wears tucked up at the place where head and neck meet. sg seemed, among his peers, thinner, of less substance. His markings were sharply contrasted: his black tail feathers very dark; his breast, very white. His slight build and distinct markings were almost certainly indications of his youth.

With his long neck and his chinstrap high behind his eyes—
almost as if it had been fastened too tightly—I was often able to
pick him out from among a dozen or so geese swimming on the
pond, sometimes even from among a greater number. On land he
was even easier to spot—he had a National Wildlife tracking band
on his left leg.

On this particular day, while SG and thirty or forty of his kith
and kin were scattered along the beach eating, the dog, who had
been chasing squirrels in the woods, came loping down the hillside toward me, to check in and to get a drink of water. The geese
turned as one and stretched out their wings to do their fast, frightened walk into the water. Startled geese may waddle rapidly toward
water, honking madly, or may lift off in flight, also honking madly.
Or they may choose this intermediate speed, if water is very near.
They flap their wings very slowly and propel themselves forward
on the tips of their webbed feet—also honking madly. This day,
when everyone turned and took off I saw that the goose right in
front of me did not spread his wings symmetrically. One wing, his
right, hung down, and its tip dragged through the sand and water
until he folded it up and swam out from shore with the others. SG's
right wing was useless. SG could not fly.

All along, all these months, he had been at the pond alone because he was not able to lift himself up into the air and join some
flock in its ever-changing triangular pattern of migration. I was
stunned by my blindness and silliness; embarrassed; confused by
questions. Most of all I was anxious with doubts about his future.
What would become of a goose who could not fly? Late in the year.
Nearly past the migratory season.

I had been trying to ensure that whatever it was I was putting
together from my time with this solitary goose was not "merely

reflections." I took photographs of SG and the other geese at the pond, throughout the beautiful New England autumn with its intense colors, its faded yellow light, its slow, teasing revelation of the unyielding infrastructure of our natural world as the leaves and flowers and bird and animal life retreat toward winter. I took photographs at the pond as one way to legitimize my presence there. I told myself I was doing a "study." I took photographs of SG so that my fixation on his presence at the pond would not seem identification, anthropomorphism, sentimental attraction.

Like other photographers of natural places, I understood the possibility that eventually the photographs would be all that was left as witness to an American landscape not thoroughly imprinted with the mechanics of human existence. In addition, I wanted to better understand how the photographic eye might influence the way we see the natural world. Yet, something about that intervening lens bothered me. As my sense of intimacy with life on the pond increased, I left the camera in the house more often. When I realized the urgency of SG's situation, the distancing lens was gone almost for good.

SG's presence on the pond was no longer an occasion for my pensive musings on solitude and isolation, on the existential loneliness of my species, and—by extension—an individual within a species. No longer could I use his solitary existence as a mystical sign affirming the spiritual "rightness" of a life I felt I had barely chosen, but had simply slipped into as a boat slips into the river current and then is moved downstream. SG was injured; his situation was not "right"—although, of course, it was perfectly natural.

As I was to learn months later, the shoulder joint of a goose is not at all like a human ball-and-socket joint. The major bone of the wing barely sits in a shallow depression of bone, and is dislodged fairly easily. SG, a young bird, may have landed on the water awkwardly and dislocated his shoulder. That would have been in late August or early September, well before I realized that his wing was dangling from its joint. During that time, the muscles that would have held the wing in place, the strong muscles that make the wings flap, propelling these large birds upward and through the sky, atrophied. A bird who does not fly for an extended period of time, especially a large bird, may not ever fly.

So, SG could not fly, and everything had changed. Because I had made him carry the burden of my meditations, because I had given him the onus of a name, because I had fed him, I could not leave him to his fate, alone on the pond.

Earlier in the season of my acquaintanceship with SG, I had telephoned some of the local wildlife rehabilitators and bird experts to find out what I should feed the goose who was often on the pond alone. Unanimously they had informed me that a solitary goose was an injured goose. I had not listened. My fiction of a correlative in the natural world was too important to be altered by fact. Besides, the advice they had given me about food, that I should try to feed the geese greens, had proven inaccurate. The geese would have nothing to do with the grass clippings and other green vegetation I worked so hard to leave for them, so I discounted their assessment of SG's circumstances.

Now, with my realization that SG was injured, it was time to admit my denseness and call the experts again to find out what to do about a Canada goose who could not fly, who was living on a pond in a woods in late autumn. These people were very patient with me, which probably comes of working with animals and having to take the time to figure out how best to help them. But they were not encouraging. There was little food left in the wild, in the environs of the pond, for the goose. On his own, he would eventually starve. Or a predator would get him, as he weakened. As long as he stayed fairly healthy and the pond did not freeze over completely he could be okay; he would be able to elude the foxes, dogs, and coyotes by escaping into whatever open water was left to him. But when the pond froze solid, any creature would be able to go out onto the ice to take him.

If I wanted to rescue him, I would have to take him out of the wild eventually. I would have to keep feeding him to keep him alive. And *I* would have to capture him; no one else was available to do this. The rehabilitator who described the process was honest with me: it is difficult to capture an adult Canada goose. Even one who cannot fly can run at a good clip, and once he gets into the water, you've lost your chance. My best chance, I was told, would be to wait just until the pond was frozen—just until that first day it was solid—then catch him by having several people form a circle around him, closing the circle little by little until someone could throw a blanket on the goose and scoop him up.

The pastoral idyll that I had been brushing in with broad strokes—at its center, the feeding of the goose—was put aside. The darkness of the shadow of mortality not only changed the lighting and the mood of the life I led at the pond, it changed the relationship of goose and woman. I still had many questions, but now they were practical. Was the food nutritious enough to keep him alive and strong? Was he eating enough, often enough, and what were the optimal times for feeding? Where should I feed him so that he would be safe? Flocks of geese eat with several lookouts on duty, so feeding time must by its nature leave them open to dangerous attacks. I wanted to know where SG was during the daytime, all those middays I had wandered over to the pond and not seen him. Was he safe there? How soon would he be absolutely alone? Would that affect him?

I needed to answer many of these questions. There was no one else to rely on. I needed to follow the goose, go to his level of seeing, let him show me how he lived. I needed to nourish the goose and my relationship with him, while the year dragged to a close in cold and darkness and all the green except the blue-green of the pines and hemlocks disappeared.

One thing I needed to know was where he was hiding at the pond. I started going over in the afternoon. I called to him. I looked everywhere I could think of that I had ever seen him—all the little inlets of the pond, the places where the trees hang down near the water. One day he stood up from his hiding place, right in front of me, and I saw how simple it was. The striking black of a Canada goose's neck and the mottled taupe of his back slip between the tall, bleached leaves and stalks that remain of the cattails late in the year. A goose can stretch out his long neck, settle down into the dry sparseness of spent vegetation, and become a part of the pattern of light and shade.

I had not seen SG in the tall grass before because I had not been looking. I looked for Canada geese in the sky or on the water, sometimes in the cornfields. Even knowing how much hunched-over geese look like a granite outcrop in a farmer's field, I hadn't thought about other forms of disguise. And, of course, the metaphors had distracted my vision. I had not wanted to envision a hiding goose. There wasn't really time for castigation. I had a mission, and it involved looking out over the world the goose surveyed—with his needs in mind, not my own.

Perhaps SG knew by the cold and the dying vegetation, by the diminished numbers of geese who flew onto the pond daily, by the lengthening darkness or the westward movement of a group of stars that looks like a flying bird. Perhaps he knew that he needed to make a connection. He stood up from the tall grass and turned his head on his long neck toward me; it had taken me a long time to look his way. He gathered himself together and turned to walk a bit, away from me. But he looked back at me, as if over his shoulder, as if making a request. And I followed.

Footprints

SG rose from the reeds to begin to show me how he lived; he looked back at me; and I followed him. I walked behind him, several feet behind him, and occasionally he would glance back to make sure I was still there. Later, that became the signal for going for a walk: he lifted himself to his feet, turned his neck to look at me, walked a few steps, looked again, then set off.

In spite of the awkward appearance of their bobbling gait, geese spend a good portion of their lives walking and can cover some distance, as one of Konrad Lorenz's staff discovered in the studies of the Greylag goose, observing a mother goose lead her goslings through the woods in her effort to return her family to the lake where she had grown up. Lorenz also studied imprinting, which, for certain species, manifests itself in animals following behind the individual who has been identified as "parent."

> One hot day in early summer . . . a very queer procession made its way through this beautiful landscape, a procession as wildly mixed as the landscape itself. First came a big red dog . . . then two men in bathing trunks carrying a canoe, then ten half-grown greylag goslings, walking with all the dignity characteristic of their kind, then a long row of thirteen tiny cheeping mallard ducklings, scurrying in pursuit. . . . At the end of the procession marched a queer piebald ugly duckling, looking like nothing on earth. . . . But for the bathing trunks and the

moving picture camera slung across the shoulders of one of the men, you might have thought you were watching a scene out of the garden of Eden.[1]

A scene from Eden: the dog, the humans, the geese, the ducks altogether, in harmony, with (apparently) one purpose. And on a summer afternoon, when the last thing anyone is thinking of is death.

When SG took me for a walk, he was showing me aspects of his life. As we walked I told him about the bird- and animal-related aspects of my life: what birds had come to the feeder and, later, how I had to thaw the ice balls from the dog's footpads with my bare hands. If only one of us understood the content of the communication, but both felt that a story was being told, that seemed to be enough.

SG walked when I was not with him. As the year grew colder, I found his footprints, frozen into the sand and the snow and the ice, showing me where he had been—telling me something of his other life, the one that wasn't just eating and hiding out. SG's tracks around the pond showed him walking a great deal: down the whole length of the pond to the bridge. Was he looking for the ducks who had once swum there? Was he hoping for a change of scenery? Up and around the wooden buildings that shelter picnickers and house the restrooms and the lifeguard room he rambled. The marks of his perambulations are the account of his solitary life. He could have been exploring. Perhaps he even left marks along the way for other geese to find and interpret. Later I collected what feathers I could find, and I took photographs of SG's frozen footprints. They make lovely arcs in the snow, and describe paths across the ice of the pond. They trace the margins of the pond, as if the goose were memorizing the details of the home he

did not mean to have, where he was lonely and cold and threat-
ened, where he had to depend upon the ministrations of a dark-
clad figure who came in the rain and the snow to scatter noise at
him even as she deliberately piled the grain.

Elizabeth Marshall Thomas introduces her study *The Hidden Life
of Dogs* with an apologia. We are massively ignorant of the lives of
these animals with whom we share so much. Her remarks seem
to imply that her main intention is to fill a void in our objective
knowledge. To some extent this is the case, although she is also
arguing that dogs are the subjects of their own lives.

> How might dogs conduct themselves if left undisturbed in normal cir-
> cumstances? No one, apparently, had ever asked.
>
> At first, that science had ignored the question seemed amazing. But
> was it really? We tend to study animals for what they can teach us
> about ourselves or for facts that we can turn to our advantage. Most of
> us have little interest in the aspects of their lives that do not involve us.
> But dogs? Dogs do involve us. They have shared our lives for twenty
> thousand years. How then had we managed to learn so little about
> dogs that we could not answer the simplest question: what do they
> want?[2]

We have learned so little because few ever thought to ask the question—much as "What do women want?" was not a question articulated until fairly recently in human history.

Thomas opens her work with a closely observed vignette, presenting a particular problem to tackle with regard to an individual
dog's life. The question she wants to answer has to do with the
travels of Misha, a Siberian husky entrusted to her. "What was
Misha doing?" when he navigated an approximately one-hundred-
thirty-square-mile range in Cambridge, Massachusetts. It is soon

clear that Thomas is also interested in *how* Misha does it—without getting hit by a car or stolen or killed—and *why*.

Thomas's inspiration is to follow Misha, on foot and on bicycle, for two or three nights a week, for nearly two years. "Right in front of me, a long-neglected gate to the animal kingdom seemed waiting to be opened. Misha held the key." Following Misha, she sees that the dog takes pleasure in his nightly prowls, in traveling through his world and communicating with the others of his species he encounters—either in the flesh or in the scents they have left behind. Following Misha leads Thomas into the dog's life, and then into the lives of the other dogs she eventually cares for and lives with. In episodic and anecdotal fashion, she tells the stories of what dogs do—when they are not involved in pleasing their human companions.

In the essay "Water Trails of the Ceriso" in *The Land of Little Rain*, Mary Austin tells of following coyotes on nightly wanderings in much the same fashion that Thomas follows Misha. Austin's goal is to apprehend something of the way in which coyotes find water in the desert, for she has observed: "The coyote is your true water-witch, one who snuffs and paws, snuffs and paws again at the smallest spot of moisture-scented earth until he has freed the blind water from the soil."[3] Like Thomas, she appreciates some special intelligence in the way in which a particular animal relates to the environment.

Like Thomas, Austin apprehends and describes the intelligence expressed through animal movement.

Watch a coyote come out of his lair and cast about in his mind where he will go for his daily killing. You cannot very well tell what decides him, but very easily that he has decided. He trots or breaks into short gallops, with very perceptible pauses to look up and about at landmarks, alters his tack a little, looking forward and back to steer his proper course.[4]

This description straddles the line between anthropomorphism and objectivity. We can see the movements of the coyote clearly, and can appreciate the use of the descriptor "proper"—denoting the fit of animal life to environment. Austin describes a being who makes considered choices. Her evidence for his mental activity is the movement, so closely described. She acknowledges that if there is a faulty intelligence it is the watcher's, who does not know enough about the coyote or his environs to know what moves his mind one way or another.

Language has always been the problem in writing the lives of animals, because mankind has established a hierarchy of consciousness with language-making (the kind that we do) near or at the pinnacle. We assume that without language, there is no story to tell. If animal lives are unexpressive, even inexpressible, then the writers who put them into words are pursuing an anthropomorphic fallacy or placing themselves firmly in a hierarchy of power and patronage, or both. They leave themselves open to charges of sentimentality and hubris. And perhaps these dangers are inescapable to a certain degree. Yet it might also be the case that we have focused too exclusively on communication, trying to decode what animals might have to *say*, to us and to each other, about their lives. What Thomas and Austin inscribe is not animal communication, but what is expressed in the animal's relationship to the natural world.

Jeffrey Moussaieff Masson and Susan McCarthy, in their study *When Elephants Weep: The Emotional Lives of Animals*, say that our vision has been too limited in our observations of animal communication: "Taught what to look for in facial features, gestures, postures, behavior, we could learn to be more open and more sensitive. We need to exercise our imaginative faculties, stretch them beyond where they have already taken us, and observe things we have never been able to see before."[5] Austin and Thomas have looked at the gestures, postures, and behavior of animals in response to each other and to their natural habitat. The sensitivities and patience of these observers make it possible for them to comprehend the individuality of response that may well express an interior landscape. Similarly, Austin reports that she has seen the coyote

> surprised by [the moon's] sudden rising from behind the mountain wall, slink in its increasing glow, watch it furtively from the cover of near-by brush, unprepared and half uncertain of its identity until it rode clear of the peaks, and finally make off with all the air of one caught napping by an ancient joke.[6]

Tom Regan's argument for the rights of animals, based on the criterion that they are subjects of a life, seems to set forth both the methodology and the reason for animal biography.[7] Most of what is credited as animal biography is writing that interjects a (human) speaking mind into the animal's subjectivity. Perhaps we could alter our understanding of "biography" and of "writing." Animals leave the marks of their lives on their environments: in the homes they build, the seeds they transport and help germinate, the trails they blaze through grass and desert, the coral they secrete—in tens of millions of ways. Animal lives are lived in a more immediate relationship to the natural world than ours. We will be able to read the stories in these relationships only when we learn to read the world better. Start by assuming that there is life out there and that some of its secrets are available to us. Some of the best places to read are in the streets of our towns at night, in the wastelands of our high mountain ranges, in parks after the fair weather is gone—in other words, at the margins of our human existence.

SG and I were both living in the margins of our species' normal spheres during those months next to a rapidly cooling pond. I followed him and paid attention to the way he lived on the pond in order to learn enough to help him stay alive. Furthermore, what I was seeing and feeling and touching along with him would provide some of the elements of his story. In addition to dramatis personae, certainly we had plot and setting. Still, what I was learning about him was how he lived in his diminished state, and in order for both SG's rescue and his story to be at all successful, I would need to draw the backdrop of normal goose life.

However, by taking even limited command over SG's environment and his story, I felt I was jeopardizing the reciprocal relationship I was hoping for. How could I express the pull SG had upon me without shaping it into a fiction of being needed—a narrative that would replace the story of his solitary state with the story of my own? I resolved to simply try to tell the story.

SG came to me, but waited for his food to be piled on the ground before he ate. Mornings and afternoons he drifted across the pond, or, later, waddled across the ice when he heard me coming. He came to me even when there were other water birds around. Some days he started eating right away, other days he seemed to think about it a while. On a few scary, very cold days, he seemed barely interested in eating, and started up to see me only to resignedly hunker down again in the snow. I was terrified he was telling me that he wasn't going to make it, and I shouldn't waste the grain.

On those days, I thought about him constantly and awoke many times in the night worrying about him. During the weeks of forming this relationship I pushed other work aside, went out twice or three times a day in fierce weather, stood at my window with brows furrowed looking out toward the pond—caught up in this bond with a Canada goose. Why?

Elizabeth Marshall Thomas tells of her desire to "enter into the consciousness of a nonhuman creature"—a desire that came from her spending late autumn afternoons with her dogs in their pen, doing nothing.[8] George Schaller, writing of time spent with Zhen-Zhen the giant panda, laments,

> Zhen and I are together yet hopelessly separated by an immense space. Her feelings remain impenetrable, her behavior inscrutable. Intellectual insights enrich emotional experiences. But with Zhen I am in danger of coming away empty-handed from a mountain of treasure.[9]

Schaller's sadness springs from believing that there is something in animal consciousness that we cannot fathom—something special, even important. A treasure. The treasure cannot be uncovered through intellectual exercise. And intellectual exercise is what we recognize as that which makes us different from, and better than, animals. Thus, why would one venture to the margins of existence, where few people believe that anything is happening, knowing that you will come away "empty-handed"? If you go there you may be in danger of losing your way, of losing the certainty of a human-centered universe. Worse still, you may lose your heart. In the conclusion to her essay "Living with Wolves"—where she is explaining the coexistence of objectivity and passion—Diane Boyd-Heger quotes Stephen Jay Gould: "We cannot win this battle to save species and environments without forging an emotional bond between ourselves and nature as well—for we will not fight to save what we do not love."[10]

When I saw SG at the pond—even now when I hear the beat of goose wings, hear their answering calls, and look up to see them patterning across the sky with their mysterious longings—I knew the thrill of an intimate knowledge of nature and the pain of knowing I will never live where I love. Animal lives are all lived at a distance from us, a distance we cannot remove. Yet, like the distance between thought and word, it is a length I am compelled to meditate on, and distance has not—by its clear air and dizzying heights and depths—lessened the longing.

The longing does not make me turn away, back to the sphere of humans within which the losses in the other, animal world only infrequently are felt as a dull thud upon the glass. Longing is neither instrument nor motive for domination or competition. While the longing to appreciate animal lives and their interrelationships with the forces of nature—the elements, the magnetic fields, the whirl of the planets, the roll of geology—will not necessarily lead to understanding or to a better relationship between the human and the animal, it is a starting point of promise. If any of us truly wants to share this earth with its nonhuman inhabitants, we will put aside hubris and put our intelligences at the service of a well-shaped desire.

One day SG came up onto the sandy beach of the pond as I stood there, and he looked straight into my eyes—suddenly I was somewhere else, in a space that exists outside of the articulations and dialectics of human life, in the rarefied space where the consciousness of the natural world breathes.

Why even try for these moments when longing is only briefly satisfied? Because there is always the possibility we will come away understanding something we need to know about the lives we live amidst the trees, next to the water, under the sky, between birth and death.

The Life of a Wild Goose

The life of a wild goose is lived in relationship to bodies of water, fields of grass or grain, and the necessary passage between these elements. Water, earth, and air. Three of the four elements, and if you consider the expense of energy required by their movement as fire, then geese might be said to be among the few, special creatures who embody a unified creation. The lives of individual geese, the makings of generations, the history of the species rolling out across the ages have always been shaped by wind and water, vegetation and climate. Of course, as is the case with most of the earth's nonhuman inhabitants, the lives of geese are also shaped by the movements of mankind on the fields, in the bodies of water, and through the flyways. The life of an individual wild goose, in this case a *Branta canadensis,* may be shaped by accidents and unique circumstances in the same way that our own lives are.

Geese have been unifying the elements in this way for a large portion of the history of the planet and over a large portion of the face of the planet. Remains of gooselike creatures have been dated to the Upper Eocene Period, which was between fifty and forty million years ago. Geese bearing a closer resemblance to the two genera to which present-day geese belong, *Anser* and *Branta*, were abroad during the Miocene Period (twenty-five million to twelve million years ago). During the Pliocene Period (twelve million to one million years ago), species within these genera came into being. In the Pleistocene Period (one million to ten thousand years ago) are found the direct ancestors of our current species. There is evidence of geese adapting to breeding on the open tundra during the Pleistocene Period, a practice still very much a part of the life cycle of migratory Canada geese: many of the *Branta canadensis* who migrate along the Atlantic Flyway breed on the tundras of Canada.

The ice ages of the Pleistocene Period are probably responsible for the multiplication of subspecies: the geese traveling in front of the ice or staying in the ice-free areas to the north formed isolated populations, and evolution took its course. Thus, *Branta canadensis* (Canada geese) exist as recognizable subspecies: the differences manifesting themselves in coloration, size, breeding territories, and migration routes. These subspecies are identified both by the Latin modification to the species name and by another label commonly recognized by ornithologists and birders. The common names have been assigned in as nonsensical a fashion as most of those given nonhuman species—names that trace back to explorers and scientists, and may only hint at some feature of the geography or physical adaptation of a living bird: Bering, Aleutian, Vancouver, Richardson, Cackling, Taverner's, Western (also known as Dusky), Moffit's, Todd's, Giant (*maxima*), Lesser, and Atlantic (*Branta canadensis canadensis*). SG fits the description of a Canada goose of the Atlantic subspecies, a group whose individuals weigh between six and eleven pounds and have distinctive white markings between the base of the neck and the back.

That which the evolving planet has shaped has also acted upon the planet. The movements of birds ensure a kind of transubstantiation in which grain in one place becomes life and energy somewhere else—the natural result of life lived between the elements. Aldo Leopold lyrically recognizes this interplay in his entry for March in *A Sand County Almanac*, sketching how, in the millennia of their movements,

> the waste corn of Illinois is carried through the clouds to the Arctic tundras, there to combine with the waste sunlight of a nightless June to grow goslings for all the lands between. And in this annual barter of food for light, and winter warmth for summer solitude, the whole continent receives as net profit a wild poem dropped from the murky skies upon the muds of March.[1]

In New England, we are more aware of the lives of geese in September, when they traditionally divide the sky with their distinctive Vs. They land on ponds and lakes, wings folding, feet stretching out, in a barely controlled chaos of intersecting angles. Yet, the control is there. I watched as somewhere between one hundred and two hundred geese landed on a pond in eastern Connecticut. Before landing, the flock separated into smaller groups, and the individuals of each group floated down toward the pond as if traveling through an invisible funnel. As each goose landed in the water, he swam off, because the next goose to descend would land very nearly in the same spot, at the base of the funnel. When one group had landed, the next began the same process, landing in roughly the same spot. As Malcolm Ogilvie explains in *Wild Geese*,

> they manage this by a technique known widely as "whiffling," which is accomplished by side-slipping first one way then the other. A skein of geese suddenly breaking up into a vertical column of tumbling, twisting bodies is a thrilling sight. There is also an accompanying tearing noise as the air spills between their widespread pinions.[2]

As coordinated as this seems, there is plenty of room for error. One goose dropping too quickly or misjudging the drift and a midair or watery collision may ensue: a likely way for a wing to get dislocated, especially if the landing goose is new to the experience.

When SG arrived on Bicentennial Pond it was an appropriate body of water for him: about one-quarter of its shoreline a green sloping lawn established and maintained by the town as an area for human usage, which had dwindled by that time of year. Unlike ducks, geese find most of their food on land. They eat eelgrass and sea lettuce and pondweed, but most of this consumption happens during the time they are nesting and raising young, when they cannot leave the water. They like grass and have developed into efficient grazing animals, cutting a field even more closely than a herd of sheep. A goose grabs hold of a few blades of grass with the front part of the bill, where there is a nail, and pulls back its head, snipping off the grass sharply. As geese have been around much longer than the trimmed greens of cultivated grass, for which most of Western culture has developed an aesthetic taste, they have a broader appreciation for, and reliance on, vegetation. They will eat

cord grass, spike rush, naiad, glasswort, bulrush, salt grass, Bermuda grass, lycium, brome grass, wild barley, rabbit-foot grass, seepweed, peppergrass, golden dock, saltbush, cattail, alkali grass, and tansy mustard. They will eat Ladino or Dutch white clover, if it is mixed with palatable grasses, but will pass alfalfa by except when young and tender. In fact, Canada geese consume so many different kinds of plants that it would seem they could survive almost anywhere. They do have favorite foods, however, and likes and dislikes seem to vary among flocks within the same general area. Some small groups may feed on pasture lands while others are feeding on stubble fields.[3]

The grasses in and near water that provide nutrition for geese in spring are less valuable as food, and less tasty, in autumn. When I first called several authorities in the area—rehabilitators and ornithologists, as well as birders I knew—to ask what to feed an injured goose, several of them (the ones who did not immediately tell me *not* to feed wild birds) suggested greens: fresh grass clippings, or discarded greens from the food cooperative where I worked every week. I tried this for about a week, distributing the largesse on the beach—where it disintegrated in the rain. I was just about to go to the library and get a book on geese, when I realized that the cow pasture I passed every time I drove to the Willimantic Food Co-op was dotted with geese.

Geese take themselves off the water at some point on an autumn morning and fly to a farmer's field that has been harvested of its corn or grain, where they glean the remaining kernels, picking them up one by one. Here is where you'll see them, if you recognize them through the camouflage. Day after autumn day, large flocks of Canada geese will spend the daylight hours in some open field, hunched over as they are eating so that it is sometimes possible to mistake them for the rocks and tufts of grass that always dot shorn fields in autumn. Except that there are always a certain number of long necks sticking up, with heads tilting first one way then the other, wary eyes checking the area for signs of danger.

Once the reason for this field of geese registered in my mind, I made the first of many trips to Thompson's Feed and Grain Store, to haul away a fifty-pound bag of scratch feed: corn and barley ground up a bit. Eventually I learned that the geese could handle this gift better if I piled the grain, rather than dispersing it; that way they got more grain per mouthful and less sand. In the morning I filled several plastic produce bags from the supermarket with grain and walked over to the pond to feed SG and whomever else was there. Sometimes I underestimated the numbers of geese and had too little to offer them. Sometimes there was only SG, and I left everything I could for him at what I had designated as safe feeding stations around the pond. The primary food area was near the water pipe, where I had found him hiding in the tall, bleached grass when he decided to let me follow him.

Any Canada goose wintering over in the temperate zones of southern New England finds himself or herself coping with a diminished world. Gradually the harvested fields become so picked over that there is little left for the geese to eat. Then, what is left freezes so that it is inaccessible to the goose. If things go well, there will be an early snowfall followed by a series of unseasonably warm, sunny days, and the snow will act as nature's fertilizer and some few new shoots of grass will come up. When this occurs, you see the geese spread out upon a sunny hillside all afternoon, reaping what the sky and the earth have sown.

The amount of food that can be gleaned has to be balanced against the flight it takes to get there. If the goose expends more energy in flying about looking for food than he acquires in the eating of that food, if home is far away or very cold, then he will die. This is one of those laws of the physical world that, like thermodynamics and gravity, we cannot dispute.

It is not only food—its decreasing availability and the increasingly slight balance of its nutritive value against the energy expended to obtain it—that transforms the outlines of the dwindling geography of the goose's world. These are also the days in which the shallow ponds and lakes that the geese need for roosting are freezing over, so he may have to go farther from the field to find an open body of water. Canada geese sleep on open water. There they are relatively safe from predators. While other birds have developed the ability to leave the muscles of their feet holding tightly to a roost while the rest of the body relaxes into sleep, or to sleep with one eye open and one half of the brain actually working at sentry level while the rest of the brain and the body rest, Canada geese are able to provide themselves protection by simply sleeping on the water, where fox and dogs cannot get at them, at a time of the day when the animal wielding a gun or a bow and arrow cannot see well enough to make a killing. Unfortunately, a larger body of water that does not freeze will also be open to winds, and a windchill factor that further lowers the goose's body temperature and depletes fat reserves. Still, the geese must have open water.

The dog and I were spending a good amount of time at the pond every day. I was still trying to do what I had set out to do: learn enough about the nature of the place to be an inhabitant. I kept track of sg, his movements and his acquaintances. Examining the water and the dirt path, the trees and the mushrooms beneath them, the plants and birds beside the pond and in it, and the sky above, I kept hoping that the scientific and taxonomic knowledge I attached to my descriptions would stick and would keep me from feeling an overwhelming sense that I was slipping through an ephemeral world.

Winter settled in early in 1996. In November we are usually tightening our coat collars around our necks, hunching our shoulders, and putting our heads down into the wind and driving rain—and there was enough of that. However, on November 11, along with a recording of fifty-nine geese and eight ducks at the pond, I noted that there were snow flurries at 1:00 p.m. The first weekend of December there was a big snowstorm: the snow was above my ankles in the morning when I went out for the paper. Although this early snow, coming during what would normally be the rainy season, was heavy and damp and sticky, there was enough of it for sledding, so my daughter and my son and his girl-friend set out for the hills across the street.

For whatever reason—heavy snow, too many little kids, not enough excitement in the incline—they left the hills between the school and the soccer field and dragged themselves and their sleds through the woods to the pond. The hill down to the pond can provide some fine sledding, especially on the south side where the spring pops out from under the hemlock tree after the ground freezes and leaves a wide sheet of ice. This is a particularly difficult area to traverse in the winter, and the dog and I usually end up making our way gingerly from one clump of reeds to the next, or going all the way up the hill, into the woods behind the spring, and circling back around to avoid having to crawl across the icy incline on hands and knees, clutching at tufts of grass for purchase.

The kids were running when they reached home, throwing open the back door and yelling for me. They had seen sG stuck in the ice on the pond and in distress. Boots tugged on, laced, coat grabbed from the closet and dragging behind me as I rushed out the door. I grabbed something to break the ice, although I could not have said at that moment what it was. I just remember having to move it from hand to hand in order to put my coat on as I tried to run, in winter boots, to the pond.

By the time I reached him, sG had gotten himself out of his pre-dicament and was hanging out in the tall grass at the bay north of the beach. I looked around at the mushy, snowy mess that was the pond and decided that he had actually been swimming in one of the last, little, partially open spots as it froze over. I used the pole

I had carried with me to break open a long channel of water just at the beach.

Open water for drinking is an absolute necessity for Canada geese. In winter, the amount of open, potable water diminishes frightfully. The small ponds, like Bicentennial, freeze in sections. Bicentennial freezes first up in the northern sections, not at the neck where water continues to flow in from the stream—even if it is very little water beneath the hillocks of ice that form above and between the rocks—but just below that, where the pond is narrow, between the inlet where geese and ducks like to hang out and the little jutting-out point where some of the best fishing seems to be. Having established a base, the ice spreads like a contagion, down the length of the east side of the pond and out into the middle. All the while more ice is forming at the southern end—between the inlet pipe for the spring and the large, concrete bulk that houses the pump, which controls the outflow and thus the level of the pond. Eventually the ice meets in the middle; then there is only a little bit of open water at the beach, at the pipe, and far up at the bridge. As the cold days labor on and the ice thickens, it is solid even at the beach and the pipe, and there are only little openings of water near the bridge, into which an industrious bird could stick his beak to get a drink.

A flock of geese can do a limited job of keeping an open space in the ice, if they have something to start with. You can see them swimming around and around their little area, as if enjoying their last bath. In fact, they are acting as avian icebreakers, trying to keep each other alive. One very cold morning, I watched a flock of geese on Bicentennial performing this task. They started to walk into the water from the shore, where they had been pecking at the last little bit of grass glistening from last night's frost. They were spread out six or seven across as usual, but as the first ones tried to slide into the water, they discovered a thin layer of ice, as brittle as the ice you can lift from a pail of water. As the first geese jammed into the ice, the ones in back got into a V formation not unlike the flight pattern. The leader had the hardest job, breaking the ice pressing against his breast. Those behind him then enlarged the path he had made. To break ice, a goose shifts his weight by pushing his legs back and up, putting the heavy, pectoral mass lower in the water and tilting the whole body forward. I could hear the ice tinkling as it broke against their feathered breasts.

sg needed open water, so I became his lead goose. While the pond was freezing solid enough for the rescue, during that period in December and early January, I made my way to a spot near the beach to unbind whatever ice had formed since my last visit. I used the handle of what had been a shovel years ago, and which we had kept in that dear Yankee fashion, knowing that someday it would come in handy for something, and guilty at the thought of discarding even such a broken-down thing. It is a sturdy ash handle—I cannot imagine how it broke—and it worked quite well for breaking ice. I held it perpendicular to the surface of the ice and brought it down as hard as I could. First a crackle would appear, then, with the (lucky) repeated blows to the same spot, the crackle would become a small hole, then a larger one. Finally I would be able to break off large chucks of ice with each blow and remove them from the pond. Ice needs the integrity of the whole for its firmness. If I left the big pieces floating in the open water, ice would re-form too quickly, so I had to get these out. Some of them came out if I flicked them from underneath with the end of the pole. Some had to be extracted by my mittened hand, which brought to my senses the cold in which sg lived.

It is intense work, breaking ice. Getting the pole to come down hard in nearly the same spot, time after time. One day I was so intent upon what I was doing, wielding the pole and banging and smashing away, that I didn't notice that I was not standing on the shore anymore. Suddenly, I brought the pole down and whap, I was standing in about two feet of ice-cold water. I made some exclamation of surprise, and the dog looked at me in wonder from her secure place on the shore. Within the minute or two that it took me to get out of the icy water, my shins were numb. I looked back at the hole to assure myself that sG had enough water for a while and I took off, calling to the dog, at a hobbled run-walk, using the pole as you would to push a punt along the Thames. Running for home and heat.

sG could not have broken enough ice by himself to keep a free spot of water for drinking. The effort alone would have cost too much of his resources. Beyond that limitation was the fact that because sG had never really practiced flight for any length of time, his pectoral muscles were not developed to anywhere near the bulk of the birds I had watched. His loss of the ability to fly not only narrowed his world to this little pond, but also severely narrowed his abilities to make a life on that pond, to contend with the elements that shape pond life. Too often, when surveying the losses the earth has had to endure, we think of only one limitation, one loss, at a time. But everything has a rippling effect, especially in a pond growing smaller.

sG continued to be cautious, even with me, even after all the months of our acquaintanceship. He acknowledged my presence, reacted to the sound of my voice, but he was discreet in his signs of intimacy or affection. And, although I ached to touch him, to establish that compelling connection between living beings that comes from touch and to experience that miracle of the immateriality of a feathered body in one's hands, I was glad that sG never suffered being domesticated, being pulled to earth in that particular way.

I see a similarity between my yearnings to caress SG and the youthful longings that Sigurd Olson felt, wanting to kill a goose. In *The Singing Wilderness* he wrote, "The sound of wild geese on the move haunted me and I felt that somehow I must capture some of their mystery, some of their freedom and of the blue distances into which they disappeared." Yet, as with my own experience, the closer Olson got to the living of the geese, the more he found himself incapable of bringing "one of those high wanderers down to earth." At the most auspicious moment for the hunter, with the geese flying overhead, the hunter's coolness disappears, replaced by the understanding, affirming vision of the naturalist.

> They were much bigger than I had ever imagined. I could not only hear the beat of their wings and the rush of air through them, but could actually feel it. At that moment they seemed almost close enough to touch and I could see their eyes, the wary turning of their heads, their outstretched feet. Then they saw me there against the rock and pandemonium broke loose. The flock climbed into the sky, beat the air desperately to escape. Not until then did I remember my gun and what I had come for, and now it was too late. The birds were out of range.[4]

Many hunters and birders have commented on the wariness of Canada geese, this quality of remaining aloof. It seems as much a part of their mystery and allure as their migrations. SG, the bird who could not fly, could retain some of this allure, could harness some of the power of his species, by keeping his physical and metaphysical distance from the human who hovered at the edges of his existence to keep him alive.

And so we went on like this, day after day, further into winter. I went to the pond with food—the cracked grain mix from the feed store—and the broken shovel handle to make a water hole in the ice near the shore. Sometimes I didn't see SG when I went over to the pond in the middle of the day, so I knew he still had places to hide. When I explained my worries about the cold and the predators to my friend Becky, we got the idea of reinforcing some of the places where he might be sheltering. I had used the last of my garden-mulching hay, so I drove to the feed store for a bale. Late one afternoon, close to dusk, I grabbed the wire cutters, a plastic bag of seed, and the icebreaker and jumped in the car. This was the first time I thought to drive the car around to the entrance to the town park, which is much closer to the pond. Somehow the walk had become part of my routine. However, that day I had too much stuff to carry. I snipped the wires on the bale and took a flake of hay with me to the pond. SG was sitting on the beach, but got up and walked carefully onto the ice as I talked to him. I explained what I was doing, and why.

I added hay to the frozen grass near the pipe where, in the past, I had fed him. Near the beach were two trash cans, close to the ice and far from the trees. I had never seen predator tracks or signs on this part of the pond. The fox, coyotes, and other four-legged inhabitants of the pond stay for the most part on the wooded side of the pond. On more than one snowy morning I had seen the fox tracks skirt the water's edge, cut across the ice, head into the trees, and come out on the playing fields that I cross to get to the pond. They were often quite fresh when I got there, so I supposed if I had wanted to catch a glimpse of the fox, I would only have had to leave the house at 5:00 a.m. But on this day I was not interested in meeting the fox, only mindful of his habits. In building a refuge for SG on the beach, I was trying to encourage him to stay away from places that might be dangerous for him.

I worried about SG because of the cold and the predators, but beneath the worry was a great sadness that he was alone. Sometimes he must have heard the other geese call as they flew overhead. No other geese came to the pond now that it was nearly frozen. I brought SG food twice a day because of the energy it took to live in the cold. The crows were eating some of the food. They didn't go to it while I was around, watching SG eat, but as I left I heard their harsh voices cut through the air and, turning, I could see them hopping closer to the food pile. I liked having the crows around and didn't mind feeding them. I hoped they might warn SG of an approaching predator in time for him to get out onto the ice, or into the last bit of water.

Ice had been forming over larger areas of the pond at night—although there were some days when warmer temperatures would free up the water—and gradually the area in which SG swam became smaller and smaller. One morning SG was sitting in the middle of the ice that was now the uniform surface of the pond. During this period when the pond was frozen over for days at a time, as we waited for the ice to thicken, it seemed to me that SG rarely left the middle of the ice. He would usually come to the shore when I broke a watering hole open for him, but if somehow that hole was still free in the morning from the evening before, he might not lift himself up from his resting position and walk across the ice for food.

That meant I had to take the food to him. Since I had watched the ice form day by day, I thought I knew where it was thickest. So one day I took the chance and walked across the ice to leave his food nearer to his resting place. The ice held, but that gave me pause, as I realized that if it held me it would certainly hold a fox, a coyote, or a wandering dog. Except for the fact that we had had little snowfall, so the surface of the ice was clear and slick—offering little purchase for fur-covered feet—SG was nearly defenseless. Yet day after day he was there, sitting on the ice, wary and watchful.

I want to call him brave, as Pattiann Rogers does the hermit crab.[5] I am trying to tell the story of SG as he lived it, the "gooseness" of it. Rogers, in far fewer words, realizes the world that a hermit crab inhabits: the sun's glare, the night's cold, the deafening noise of the waves beating on the shell home of the creature who holds on "day after day after day." What does it mean to call this bravery, when we know (don't we?) that the animal's behavior is instinctive, that in fact he does not make a choice to hang on to the rock through "pistol-shot collisions [his] whole life long" or to hang on to a continually diminishing existence in a world of icy surfaces—dead reed stalks cracking in the wind and cold, months after the last bird call?

Yet I have seen the geese who did not hold on to life in the cold. One January morning, nearly two years before SG landed on Bicentennial Pond, I discovered a goose frozen into the pond, down near the embankment, close to the brittle reed stalks. The goose's head was bowed, the beak frozen into the ice, the neck forming a poignant arch against the blue-gray of the ice. It was as if the head had grown too heavy, as sometimes happens with a child who slumps into sleep in a sitting position. A week later, animals dragged the carcass out of the water and ate it—leaving a spray of feathers for the wind.

Ice

That winter of SG I was surprised to discover how frightened I was of the ice. I was afraid to walk on the ice, but that fear might be ascribed to my having fallen hard on an icy patch of road several winters before. I cracked a vertebra and spent several days unable to do more than walk from one part of the house to another, in between naps on the red couch. Of the dual specters of pain and limitation, I think I am more afraid of limitation.

I was afraid of the booming and cracking noises the ice made. Noises that filled up the space above the pond. Space that was so still in winter, with all birdsong except that of crows silenced. The booms and cracks were unexpected, the source of the noise undefined.

Did I perceive the booming and cracking as a prelude to ice breaking and to my falling through? The threat of falling through the ice had been used to circumscribe some of my tomboy childhood. Yet now that I had had some experience with falling through breaking ice, these fears should have been allayed. (The dog had fallen through the ice and into the pond, and I had dragged her out and gotten her home safely. And there was that time I had fallen in up to my knees, when I was careless breaking the ice.)

Since I had to be next to the ice every day, and had to walk across it often, I spent some time trying to analyze this fear in order to put it aside. I find that analyzing fear, as I have been doing here, rarely works to lessen it. You end up with an even longer list of things to be afraid of. What sometimes works is peeling the fear as if it were an onion. Just sort of mentally wearing it down.

As it happens I am not afraid of ice. I am afraid of the dark world below the ice.

Even though the world below the ice, I tell myself rationally, is some version of the world of mussels and algae, of fish and toads and turtles, of brown mud and brown rotting leaves that I see every day as I look at the pond in spring and summer and fall—that same world captured by ice and locked away from my examination is frightening.

The ice can be explained by physics and chemistry. Just a few equations describe the transformation of water to ice. They are not simple equations, however, as I discovered when I tried to use scientific knowledge to wave away my fear. The ways that ice forms, especially in the wild, on ponds and lakes with uneven bottoms and water sources that remain unfrozen, are complex enough to be the subject of entire books. Ice forms in layers, too, and the existence of previous layers affects the way that ice continues to form. Like so many aspects of the natural world, once a process gets started, it continues according to different forces that are increasingly hard to separate, to describe, to exercise any control over—whether it is the control of letter or number.

Ice is hard: hard to explain, hard to describe. Its hardness seems to be the cessation of the animation that is water. It has the stillness of death. Dead things were frozen into the ice, leaves and seeds and grasses. The occasional dead goose. It is possible that things that had been living up until the point of freezing were in the ice, although I never saw examples of these. In February I did not see frozen fish bobbing like exotic ice cubes in the reanimated water. Yet it was possible that there was death beneath me, hidden beyond the thin layer of clarity, beyond the obfuscating bubbles and the darkening impurities in the ice.

Yet, even as I began to understand the images and associations that made ice funereal, I understood another aspect of its immobility. History was suspended in the pond. The past was in the ice: the past of the pond and the past of my experience with sg. I could read that history in the footprints that decorated the margins where the bluish ice met the whitish snow, next to the crackling reeds. What was frozen was the past of the living pond that I remembered.

The present wasn't really there. Neither sg nor I left very much of an impression as we walked across the pond those last cold days. I suppose my feet tamped down the snow a bit, but I wasn't making much of an impression on the ice. However, when this present ice melted, it would take with it sg's footprints and most of the witness of his presence.

If I swept the snow aside and looked down into the ice, I saw air bubbles scattered so randomly that they might have been stars in a very crowded sky. Sort of a light-on-white version of the Milky Way. And, like the stars of the Milky Way, the air bubbles enticed my vision into the darkness beyond and behind. There was the nothingness that I was afraid of. We glide through the darkness or are captured for a moment like the air bubbles in the ice on a pond in winter.

When we think of what is out there—"on stars where no human race is"—we reflect on our insignificance, the brevity of individual life.[1] I did not want to have these thoughts—of the indifferent darkness beneath my feet, just on the other side of a glass I could quite possibly pass through, as Alice did through the looking glass—every time that I set foot upon the ice to take SG his food or to go walking with him.

Yet I did. I did not make the fear dissipate by waving equations and poetry at it. Every time I set foot on ice I feel that great, sweeping darkness beneath my feet waiting to take me. A great sweeping that is all that I cannot understand or fathom in the universe, but whose presence I must accept. Now I walk on ice, still in fear, but also grateful for the opportunity to be in that presence. As I walk I revel in the chance to see a world that might seem familiar in a changed, and charged, perspective.

Never Underestimate the Animal

Usually, on our walks, SG would take me along the edge where the grassy or snowy slope met the pond. Or we meandered up the beach. Sometimes he took me onto the ice, although I am loath to go there. I told him how little I like to walk on ice, how scared I am of the cracks and booms beneath my feet. Beneath the ice the pond has a secret life, too "other" for my comfort. Yet I walked out onto the ice, telling my fears to a solitary goose. When we walked I tried to take care not to step on his prints, for I knew that soon they would be all I would have left of him at the pond.

By mid-January SG seemed tired of his lot; he rarely left the soft center of the ice. On a Thursday it rained—that cold, hard, dark gray rain of a New England winter. The radio weather forecast was for a cold snap with subzero temperatures at night and daytime highs only in the teens. It was time to get SG off the ice.

On Friday, December 20, 1996, the Hartford *Courant* ran the headline "Bald eagle suffering from lead poisoning after ingesting lead shot" on the front of the "Connecticut" section. The large photograph accompanying the article showed the staff of the Kensington Bird and Animal Hospital in Berlin. I had cut the article from the paper after reading it and called the hospital for advice on SG. I was immediately connected to Scott Kolpa, a veterinary assistant, who talked me through the process of rescuing a bird from the wild. Later I would find out that this talk is given over and over by those who field questions about wild birds.

Over the phone, Scott recited the protocol I later saw in the wild-life rehabilitator's handbook. What Scott told me I absorbed as bits of information, the elements I could process and retain long enough to do what must be done. It was necessary to have a plan. It was necessary to have quiet, to move gently and stay calm. I should avoid eye contact as it might seem threatening. I should protect myself with gloves, glasses, and thick clothing. I was to guide rather than chase. The goal was to cover the goose with a blanket or towel, keeping the sharp claws and strong beak tucked in. Once I had him in some secure container for transport, I would take him to Scott. Everyone who spoke with me about the rescue of injured wildlife gave the same parting advice: *Never underestimate the animal.*

To capture an injured bird, you need as many people as it takes to make a large circle around it. You need one or more blankets to throw over the bird—apparently the dark and the weight of the blanket make the bird quiet and minimize possibly self-injuring flappings. You need at least one person to be calm and make the final decisions.

That Thursday in January, I stood in the rain and talked to sg about the cold that was coming, about being caught, about being taken someplace warm and safe where someone would look at his wing. I made no promises to sg or myself about flight. I went home and called Scott.

The veterinary hospital would only be open until noon on Saturday, but it would be open on Monday, a holiday. The holiday was perfect because my children and their friend who was going to help would not be in school, and my women friends could use the holiday to put off going to work. Monday is perfect; I tell Scott to expect us. Meanwhile, it was raining and slush was collecting over the old ice. I didn't know how long it would take to refreeze. The ice had to be solid, because at the very least I would have to walk out onto the ice to guide SG into the circle. Monday had to be it. But it was so far away from Thursday, across such an expanse of cold and danger.

At least talking to Scott had been reassuring. There were positive thoughts to focus on. The cold would limit predator activity. SG would be in good hands after we took him from the pond. After repeating Scott's instructions back to him, I didn't even hang up the telephone, but pressed the buttons and started the other calls: to the rescuers. Silently I repeated that I was not crazy to be doing all this for one wild life.

Friday, Saturday, Sunday. Everything I did that weekend had as backdrop my awareness of cold and my knowledge that something would end on Monday. I would get to hold SG, briefly, but then he would be gone.

Saturday morning I started thinking about herding a goose. SG was in his drainpipe nest, so I went down to the beach and, instead of walking around the pond, stepped out onto the ice, about eight to ten inches in his direction. I had never been the one not on the land, and SG seemed a bit nonplussed, but not frightened. He moved his head to one side, then the other, but did not get to his feet. He seemed to accept my presence; after all, it was very cold and I was feeding him. I repeated this exercise in the afternoon. On Sunday morning I brought a blanket and crossed the ice carrying it—talking, as usual. I stood five feet away from SG, on the ice, telling him some story for a while. Then I started to unfold the blanket. He was up and bobbing away in that curious, staid, one-foot-in-front-of-the-other manner. The blanket had spooked him, and that was going to be a problem. Sunday afternoon I only carried the blanket, not unfolding it, so he would at least be prepared to see me with something bulky.

There was straw in the kennel, and it was in the back of the van. There were blankets by the back door. Everyone had his or her instructions. After a night of little sleep, I left early to herd SG up onto the beach, to talk to him, hoping that my familiar voice would keep him from freaking at the appearance of so many other people. And I wanted to spend the extra time with him.

I made a big pile of food on the beach, then walked onto the ice to rouse SG from his snug spot near the drainpipe. We walked in parallel tracks toward the beach: he was on land; I was on the ice. He ate quickly and settled down again. I had been talking to him, saying good morning, telling him to eat. I had told him what was going to happen—as much as I could, considering that I was having trouble visualizing the process. There were seven people and four blankets, and only one chance to do this, or SG would be so spooked he would never come near me again.

So there I was, standing on a frozen pond at eight in the morning talking in a soothing fashion to a Canada goose nestled on some snow-covered sand a few feet away. I told him about the other birds I feed: the backyard birds. I named as many as I could, because a list of names is almost always mesmerizing. I told him how much I respected him for having survived the way he had. (These are the things I remember saying, although I was talking for quite a while and must have covered several other topics.) Finally he seemed still, and I ventured to unfold the blanket. Nope, he didn't want to see that blanket, and he was walking up the hill. I stuffed the blanket under my arm and took off alongside him, not wanting him to get into the woods where it would be very difficult to encircle him. I got in front of him and herded him back downhill, trying to stay between him and the ice.

However, at this point the rest of the group arrived, and as I tried to move SG toward them, he got frightened and, using his poor misshapen wing, skated and skidded onto the ice. I was still talking. When that morning unrolls in my mind's eye, I see myself talking without ceasing throughout the whole wild goose chase. I never took my eyes off SG, in fact I felt as if in a trance, totally focused on maintaining the connection between Sydney and the goose. There were only the two of us on the ice. I had never walked across the ice to the middle of the pond, and SG looked back at me when I did. I herded him back onto the beach, and he spooked again.

I remember walking out onto the ice three times. The ice boomed; I heard that, but my focus damped down the fear. I shuffled across the slickness like a deferential woman, head bowed to keep my eyes on a walking goose, moving as if I had been visited by the footbinder. Constant moving; constant talking. Onto the ice and off. Up the hill and down. SG stayed four feet away—too far for me to throw the blanket on him—looking back at me, wondering at my stubbornness. After a while I could hear my husband saying, "You'll have to do it; you'll have to cover him." But if I moved to open the blanket, SG scurried away. Then we were up on the hill again and I was thinking we would have to go back down, but out of the corner of my eye I saw the circle forming.

And then SG turned. He turned right toward me. Came right at me, fussing a bit, but mostly quietly. Head up and looking right at me. I threw the blanket over him. It worked just as the wildlife people had said: he was absolutely still and I held him through the blanket while my son retrieved the kennel. There was nothing to him—he was so light, so insubstantial. What bulk I had seen must have been the air in the down of his feathers, because in my hands it was like holding only the blanket. When I had him inches from the open kennel door, I pulled back the blanket and saw that he had his head under his sorry wing. It only took a little push to get him into the kennel.

It was over, and I felt like I was breathing mountain air. The insubstantiality had passed from my hands to my chest to my soul. It had gone well. SG was not hurt and did not even seem too discomposed in the blanket-covered kennel. There was a whirlwind in my mind, but those were things for my mind. This was a time to think about SG. It was the end of this part of his story.

A Bird Who Cannot Fly

The Kensington Bird and Animal Hospital is a small storefront in a strip mall on the busiest road in Berlin, Connecticut. At the receptionist's desk I signed in SG on a yellow pad specifically for wild birds. A large sign on the desk declared that wild birds were treated free of charge. I had called as we left the house, so we were expected. Scott came out to the reception area, introduced himself, picked up the kennel, and turned to go back into the working part of the hospital. I didn't know the protocol, but I followed. I was, after all, the "mother of the patient." Loose parrots and parakeets gazed at me from perches and file cabinets and flew through the exam areas.

We released SG into a clean stall, where he had more straw, a towel, some water, and food pellets. I reached into my pocket and discovered that I still had some of the scratch feed, so I gave that to him, too. He was safe and warm and had food. There were other birds in the immediate vicinity. He wasn't hissing, and his carriage was normal—stately. He was looking at me as I told Scott a brief version of his story and gave a report on the rescue. Scott had work to do; my husband was waiting in the reception area. I said good-bye to SG.

I finally allowed myself to cry in the car on the way home. In the car, my husband, Terry, mentioned that SG seemed to be moving much less well than he had a month previously. For the most part he was dragging his wing, and that had made him quite lop-sided. Before he had been able to tuck it up next to him, and sometimes he could even beat it in the air a bit for some extra velocity. Terry's observation was a portent. When the phone call from the office reached us later in the day, the report from the veterinarian was that SG had a dislocated shoulder and muscles so atrophied that flight would never again be possible. The folks at Kensington would have to send SG to one of their permanent placements, not to a rehabilitator.

I should have felt relieved that SG would always be safe from predators and cold, from hunger and loneliness. But he would never fly overhead in a swiftly shifting V. He would never tilt his wings, adjust his primary feathers, and skid and splash into a pond. In particular, he would never again be on Bicentennial Pond. Most people will believe that SG could not experience this loss. Still, there are those who feel differently. Unfortunately, I am one of them.

On the Wednesday after the Martin Luther King holiday, SG was taken from the Bird and Animal Hospital to his new home: the Hungerford Outdoor Educational Center, part of the New Britain Youth Museum at Hungerford Park, right down the road from the vet. On Friday I called to check on him and to introduce myself to anyone I could find who might be indulgent enough to let me talk about my relationship with this goose. Actually, everyone was willing to talk to me, but I finally ended up speaking with Joe, because he was the person who cared for the big birds at Hungerford. Joe even seemed excited to learn that the goose responded to human talk, had seemed to respond to his "name." He promised to go try this out as soon as we were done on the telephone. Then he told me which cage SG would be in for two weeks—he had to be in isolation because he was coming in from the wild—and gave me the hours when he himself would be at the center.

Both the vet and Joe seemed convinced that SG had to be a female because of "her" small size. From the very beginning of my recognition that a lone goose was a continuing presence at the pond, I fell into the habit of referring to SG as "he." At that time, my dog and I were walking around the pond one or two days a week with a friend, Donna, and her dog: two women, two female dogs. When I told Donna that I was monitoring a solitary goose, pointing SG out to her, she immediately began referring to SG as "she." For a while, I pointedly corrected her in conversation. In fact, it is very difficult to distinguish the *Branta canadensis* gander from the goose. I read somewhere that the head of the male was more triangular in shape, but I think this piece of knowledge falls into the category of folklore. Donna never changed her appellation, and after a while I stopped trying to use the correction as a speech act to establish my proprietary rights.

However, this difference in gender determination was one of the first things that got me thinking about SG in a more analytical fashion. That Donna called SG "she" included the goose in our little group, in which women and dogs took turns seeming to understand each other, as we walked and talked along the trail through the woods. My gender determination of SG, on the other hand, seemed a result of my impulse to view SG as the "other"—either a subjective figure of animal presence or an object of study. My mind articulated the space between us as deeply as it could—by ascribing it to a difference in gender. If I had been thinking of SG as female, as a "sister," I would have been emphasizing the aspects of nurturing and caring, my concern for "her" safety. In the months of talking to SG, following him around the pond, responding to his hanging on to life and his fragile independence, I had identified him as a male. It was a part of my willing him to survive. It is ironic that someone with pioneer women in her background would make the assumption that the male would be the survivor. However, whatever bias this reveals, it seemed to me preferable to the prevailing, patronizing attitude toward animals, which assumed they were all weaker than humans. I wanted to feel SG as a presence of equal weight in the universe, even though I had to have much thicker ice beneath my feet to stay above the dark cold.

Rescuing SG, holding him and carrying him, gave shape to the emotions that are a part of the heart of nurturing, and of love. Taking SG from the wild had the possibility of changing my feelings about him, making me acquiesce to the "change" in gender. But it didn't. Before I left SG at the vet on that Monday afternoon in January 1997, I wrote down the numbers on his band. My son, of the sharp eyes and excellent numerical recall, had already read them off to me, but I wanted to be sure. 878-62857. When you find a banded bird, you are supposed to contact the Department of the Interior, especially if you have a report of a change in life or lifestyle for that bird. After SG went to live at Hungerford, I contacted the U.S. Department of the Interior, U.S. Geological Survey, Biological Resources Division, Bird Banding Laboratory in Laurel, Maryland. In return for my information on the whereabouts of 878-62857, I was issued a Certificate of Appreciation, with SG's banding data. He was banded near Willington, Connecticut, a town just to the north, on July 1, 1996. Age of bird: "too young to fly when banded." Sex: Male. I keep the certificate in a plastic envelope with the feathers and the bits of seed I picked up on the beach the day after we rescued SG from the pond.

During the months of caring for SG at the pond, in contacting people to ask for guidance, I learned something about the work of wildlife rehabilitators in Connecticut. I was for a while drawn into the circle of hands that mend the wings, fix the broken legs, and feed the orphaned young of beings who live in the wild. Wildlife rehabilitation is work of a special kind of magic, of a different kind of power that has nothing to do with control and domination. It is work that stresses, above all else, the preparation of the animal or bird for life in the wild. It is not domestication, not a bringing of wild life into the human sphere. Even though the animals and birds are often brought into human homes during their rehabilitation, practitioners go to great lengths to reproduce the animal's habitat in a smaller, safer place. The birds and animals are encouraged, even forced, to learn how to live on their own, in the wild.

Caring individuals have been trying to help distressed animals probably for as long as we have been occupying the same space. But only in the last thirty years has significant attention been paid to gathering information on wild animal lives, their anatomy and nutrition, and their injuries and diseases and the treatments of these. Wildlife rehabilitators go through a course of training, serve an apprenticeship, and take a test given by the Department of Environmental Protection in order to become licensed. Then they donate their resources of time, energy, and money to provide "the treatment and temporary care of injured, diseased and displaced indigenous wildlife and the subsequent return of healthy animals to appropriate habitats in the wild."[1]

Although, as the rehabilitator's manual asserts, "wildlife biologists and conservationists view animals as members of dynamic and interacting populations,"[2] wildlife rehabilitators most often do their work one animal at a time. And sometimes their work seems never to end. One rehabilitator, who specializes in working with skunks, but who also works with raccoons, related this story about a raccoon she called Larry, who had been rehabilitated from an injury and then released:

Larry kept coming back when he got into trouble. For example, one time I found Larry outside our raccoon pen, bloody & covered with puncture wounds. I thought he was dead. But his eyes blinked. That resulted in a quick trip to the vet & 3 weeks of antibiotics, each time Larry tried to bite off my hand when I had to give him an antibiotic shot. He had such a foul temper! Finally, after 3 weeks, he was released again. No sign of Larry for weeks. Then on Thanksgiving, Larry appeared with a fishhook stuck through his nose! Again, a trip to the vet . . . all the while Larry biting & snarling. Finally we released him. Six weeks later, Larry appeared with a broken leg. True to form, Larry tried to bite us as we put him in a carrier to go to the vet's! We treated him (which was no picnic!).[3]

Rehabilitation is the work done to make the animal fit for life independent of human (or nonmutual) nurturing. As Irene Ruth has expressed it, her goal is to make sure her charges can "go out and get jobs being animals."[4] Larry apparently wanted to have his cake and eat it, too.

Some rehabilitators are incorporated into nonprofit organizations. However, most are volunteers who have been drawn to the work of caring for demanding newborns, treating injuries, providing suitable habitats for growth and learning, and teaching life skills as best they can—with the end in mind of watching as the hawk soars into the sky, the skunk waddles off into the undergrowth. Work without pay, generally without acknowledgement from society, and often without notice from the one who benefits from the care. It is work that requires an enormous emotional commitment and is meant to end as suddenly as it begins.

There are many points at which wildlife rehabilitation may be compared to human nurturing, aside from the obvious: long hours, terrible pay, and social marginalization. However, there is one outstanding difference: a rehabilitator must sometimes make the decision to put an injured animal to death, when in her judgment that animal can be neither healed nor sent into an educational program nor used for captive breeding.

The people, mostly women, who nurture animals are like those who nurture other humans in that, due to their diminished economic status, they are politically, socially, and psychologically unobserved. The greater portion of the community does not see what rehabilitators do, nor do they see (nor wish to see) wildlife. The work rehabilitators do is necessitated by the predominance of a human culture thoroughly steeped in and dependent upon the mastery, or possibly the eradication, of the natural world.

Perhaps in this work of nurturing, in the actions and exchanges of wildlife rehabilitators—and of all nurturers—can be found the seeds of change, an incipient insurrection, an as yet unspoken and unwritten ethos or mythos, the unconscious or subconscious motivation of which is to change the way that we treat animals, and, eventually, the way that we live on this earth.

To look at the work of women wildlife rehabilitators is also to explore how we make amends: how we take the animals into our sphere, and then return them to theirs. Wildlife rehabilitation in some ways mirrors our relationship to the environment and can certainly suggest the shape that restoration may take.

Nurturing. The giving of what is required—one hopes with compassion and patience—by one who has, to one who needs. How can that be rebellion? How can that pattern be anything other than the same old pattern of human patronization of animals, seen as lesser beings in intelligence, emotion, and ability to act upon the world? In the case of wildlife rehabilitation, the intersection of human and animal worlds is predicated on the animal's being injured, or young, or somehow unable to perform his or her function as animal, a situation that would seem to enhance the distance between the two consciousnesses and encourage stratification into the hierarchy of healing, of stewardship.

However, the work of wildlife rehabilitation emphasizes empathy, "the ability to visualize oneself in the same situation as the animal."[5] Rehabilitator Taunya A. Netich recalls,

> When I was about 6 years old we kept a kitten that couldn't walk due to brain damage. The vets all advised [us] to put the little stray to sleep, but we taught the cat to walk, and climb into a chair to see out the window, and he lived for 13 years about as normal as any other cat. "Whiskers" taught me early on how to be compassionate and have patience with a disability.[6]

Many hours of physical training were needed to get a disabled cat to climb onto a chair. This accomplishment testifies to the patience necessary for this work and exemplifies the compassionate vision of many in this field. Taunya and others like her recognize that the object of training should be to get the cat onto the chair to see out the window, because that is what someone who had observed the behavior of cats would choose as the appropriate goal. The radical aspect of this story, and of the work of rehabilitators, is their choice to view the situation through the eyes of animals and with that vision to create the chair-and-window world.

That adaptation of vision, from accepting a version of animal life to understanding how the animal really lives, is part of the transformative nature of wildlife rehabilitation. Actions like this, and the stories that come from them, have the ability to change the nurturer, who otherwise is perceived as not needing to be altered. The transformative power works in a circular pattern. It is not possible to prevent wildlife from further injury—and habitat loss and degradation, poisoning from pesticides, death by automobile when roads are laid across animal pathways—without acquiring the ability, and then the habit, of experiencing the world as the animals who live in it do.

The transformative power of nurturing is one of the aspects put forward by Luce Irigaray as part of an ethic of nurturing.[7] Irigaray's motive is to illuminate nurturing as a (might we say, natural) process, removed from the disfiguring constraints of patriarchal society. She puts forth two principles for the development of a feminist ethic of nurturance: that the power exercised by the nurturer be "primarily healing, creative, and transformative" and that the relationship between nurturer and nurtured be not only symmetrical, "but at least potentially mutual and reciprocal."[8]

Irigaray's work is shaped by the nurturing relationship of human mother and daughter. Several of the wildlife rehabilitators who told me their stories acknowledged that their first experience at "rehabilitation" had been raising a litter of young animals whose mother had been killed. Sometimes this experience occurred when the woman was herself little more than a child—providing an opportunity for the child to be transformed into a mother, someone to whom other lives have been entrusted, by choice or by fate.

Even though rehabilitators are warned about the emotional danger of naming animals who are to be released, it is a fairly common practice. It would almost seem unavoidable, if one is preparing for the inevitable individuation of the one being nurtured. This practice would seem to make nurturing animals even more like human nurturing.

It has often been presumed that women have a greater empathy with animals because of their mutual position of "otherness." However, as Irigaray describes it, in human nurturing the

"Otherness of the infant is wounding to both" nurturer and nurtured. The patriarchal concepts of necessary separation of mother and (female) child lead to confusion about identity in both, which Irigaray sees as creating a double bind, in which neither mother nor daughter can act—thus the title of her article translates as "And the One Doesn't Stir without the Other." Without a positive, life-affirming definition of nurturer, the one fulfilling that role tends to disappear into the one nurtured, who is only the product of an act, not an individuated entity.

Perhaps wildlife rehabilitation is, instead of a pale copy of human nurturing, a more positive model. For, unlike human mother and daughter, the wildlife rehabilitator and the animal she cares for do not fill the same space either within the culture or in the physical world. One does not have to be supplanted for the other to grow.

Of course, the mutuality of a relationship between human and animal, especially an injured or domesticated animal—but really any animal—is problematic. A human's recognition of an animal's individuality may easily become mired in attachment, in which it is not the animal's identity that is recognized, but the traits we wish upon him. Furthermore, it is difficult to recognize the animalness of an animal while keeping the relationship symmetrical—that is, not introducing hierarchies of power that completely undermine mutuality. Still, when I heard Jayne Amico tell a story about a rehabilitated hummingbird who returned to her backyard to buzz her backside, I thought the story an example of reciprocity, not dominion.[9]

If this nurturing and healing is taking place all around us, why do we have so few stories, so few empathetic visions of the lives of animals? Because, as feminists have theorized, the silence surrounding nurturing is a result of economic scarcity. There are rarely enough hours in the day to do the work and to write it down. The political, economic, and social construction of nurturing have muzzled it, recognizing its rebellious nature. The real danger is not in the bark, nor the bite, of the nurturer, but in her continued silence. In silence the earth will be paved over. We must tell the stories of wounded and orphaned animals, of caring for them, listening to them, learning from them, connecting to them, accepting their trust as the gift it truly is. We can begin the process of repairing the earth and our relationship to it. What is handed from mother to child and back again, from rehabilitator to skunk or goose and back again, is life. Writing about one of her experiences in bird rehabilitation, Linda Hogan expresses the value of this effort and its necessity:

> As women we have especially tried to protect them, for maintaining life seems to be our feminine work. And we know, remember, that when we return to our relationships with the animals, it is not just the animals that we begin to restore, but our own place within the dynamic of life. The human soul, too, in its feminine form, as anima, is restored along with the other life-forms. With it, we find the deepest meaning of what it is to be human, and how we are meant to live in this godly world.[10]

The rehabilitator's motto is sometimes expressed as, "What could possibly be better than flying free?" SG was not flying free. If I believed the words of the experienced veterinarian and the rehabilitators who had seen him, and there was no reason not to, he would never fly. But flight is what birds are all about; it is how we define them. Flightless birds are an aberration: they are either quizzical oddities, like ostriches and emus, or domesticated factories for food we do not even consider to be birds anymore. It is hard to know what to make of a bird who cannot fly. Or, stated less delicately, it was hard not to see a flightless SG as less than a bird, a vehicle for my longing, a creation of my need and imagination.

One wanders into this particular slough of despond hampered by the blinders of the cultural misconceptions inherent in the paradigm. I keep pulling and picking at these blinders, keep trying to see more clearly SG on the pond.

If I were to accept that only an SG who could fly—after my protecting him from predators and the elements and making sure he got the proper medical care for his wing—validated my experience and his life, I would empty of meaning the months on the pond, the habits of caring, the knowledge gained, the moments when something happened between us. I would be accepting—worse yet, I would be imposing upon SG—a limiting definition of "bird": The one who can fly. This is the identity based upon human evaluation. It is a valuation based upon "use" just as our value for chickens is; but the use is metaphorical rather then economic (or gastronomic).

Flight is still a mystery, even in the century after the Wright brothers—and migration is proving to be almost impenetrable. Birds who fly provide us with this sense of mystery, the sense of wonder, which is a mainstay of our response to the natural world. It is not that I want to take away that sense of wonder. The wonder of human observers is probably what stands between Yellowstone the national park and the same land as parking lot or development. However, it is one thing to value wonder and another to believe that the purpose of the nonhuman world is to provide us with energies and sensory experiences to move us to wonder. Wonder is a valuable part of who we are. Birds have their own purpose in flying. To say that birds have to fly in order to have a place in the world is to say that birds have value only as they fulfill us. This is the same anthropocentric, hierarchical vision of the natural world that gets us into trouble all the time.

Furthermore, if I were to accept this view of my time with SG, devaluing it because of the nonconforming outcome, I would also be devaluing the process of nurturing. The overwhelming majority of wildlife rehabilitators are women; they are doing women's work. It is the dreary work of caring: not the dramatic and heroic work with the scalpel and the prescription pad, the MRIs and the CAT scans, but the daily work of preparing food and cleaning up feces and looking out for the dangers against which there are prophylactics (and using maternal juju against the other dangers).

Nurturing places us in a participatory relationship with the earth. This is something different from the paradigm of dominion, which frames rehabilitation as using human abilities to return animals to the way of life we have determined is correct for them: "We know what is best for you." Even in the care of a truly gifted rehabilitator, it is not always possible for the animal to be "free" from a constrained life, from human intervention. Yet it is the case that the otherness of the animal always remains free and clear, whether we recognize this aspect of the world's largesse or not.

Maybe it is precisely these animals who live in between who need their stories told. In reviewing some of the stories told about animals, Marian Scholtmeijer says, "Establishing the legitimacy of outcast experiences is precisely the political cultural work that needs to be carried out in real life for the sake of all beings disenfranchised by sanctioned value systems."[11] Accepting the animal nature of the animal in captivity, the animal who cannot live his genetically imprinted life, is extremely difficult. It is also difficult for us, humans, the ones with the tools and the interfering tendencies, to accept what we cannot fix, cannot change.

SG was a bird who could not fly, and it was hard to find the page that described him in any of my bird books. It was hard to find the name that properly described our relationship or, in describing it, gave credit to his presence. And perhaps I did not want to put a name to the force that pulled me across the state every ten days or two weeks, in snow and rain. I continued to visit SG at the Hungerford Outdoor Educational Center, where I followed him into the next stage of his bird life.

Wild Poems

I continued to visit the pond, to watch the geese and other birds—
even though SG was not there, even though there was no special
need for my presence. Or perhaps there was: I was still the connection between SG and the wild. All the news from the pond I
took to him on my visits, repeating my observations (however inaccurate) so that we would not forget his claim on life.

15 March 1998

*The snow collapses from the trees, exhausted from trying to hold
on while the sun and a softer wind do their mid-March work.*

*The geese bathe themselves by rocking into the water—their long
necks begin the movement, establish the rhythm, and they rock hard
enough to partially submerge & to send small waves up over their
wings and back. Then, upright again, the goose ceases the rhythm &
then each neck bends around to poke at the gland where the lifesav-
ing oils are held, and these are spread about some. The last act in the
bath "theater" is a triumphant and noisy rearing up, wings beating
in the air—loud thumping whooshes.*

30 March

*The Canada geese are missing from the pond. For 2–3 weeks I've
been feeding the geese, as I used to feed SG—in part because I wanted to gain enough familiarity that I would be able to find their nests*

without scaring them. For the last 10 days or so there have been 2 pair of geese and about 6 miscellaneous geese, as well as 2 pair of ducks. Today only one male mallard had the clear water, rippled gently by the wind, to himself. I fed him and he stuck next to the beach. As I circumambulated the pond, checking to make sure the geese were gone (not hiding), I heard a rustle in the tall grass near where SG *used to hide. I think the female duck is in there on her nest. The male waited until I had left the hillside, then swam out to the middle of the pond, trying not to look toward the tall grass near the inlet pipe. I tried to be quiet & invisible, just at the top of the hillside, but he didn't make a move toward the grass. I'll keep trying to spy him changing places with the female. I'll also start putting food on* SG's *"beach" near the pipe, so she won't have so far to go.*

According to Stokes, incubation is 28 days, which puts the eggs hatching just after the beginning of fishing season (if the eggs were just laid). I'll need to keep an eye on this situation.[1]

My journal entries betray ignorance and insight, wistfulness and a hope based on some knowledge of the nature of things. What I was watching, on the fifteenth of March, was not geese bathing—but geese mating. If I had stayed around for another thirty minutes, I might have seen the male mount the female. But I had work on my desk, and something in my heart was resisting making another attachment to the geese of Bicentennial Pond.

The ducks came back in February; the geese, in March. The pussy willows came into being, then into flower. The swamp azaleas flowered with their feet in the pond. I had just begun thinking about kingbirds, reveling in the predictability of the world around the pond, when I was surprised. The week of my fiftieth birthday I went over to the pond as usual one morning and there were four yellow-and-olive-gray gatherings of down floating between the two geese I had seen there earlier in the spring. The geese had kept a nest hidden from me and from the fishermen and had managed to incubate and hatch four goslings.

Goslings are precocial and nidifugous—they hatch with eyes open, ready for action, able to leave the nest. At only one day old they are led by their parents to the safety of open water. For many geese, this is simply a matter of traveling a few feet, but for some there is an overland journey of ten miles. Any travel on land is slow and fraught with dangers. Precocial hatchlings are covered with down, which in the case of goslings is not entirely waterproof. So the parents must waterproof the goslings before that initial swim. Even being hatched with independent abilities does not mean a gosling can survive without parenting.

The parents lead the goslings into the water in formation, with the gander usually taking the lead and the goose keeping everyone in line from the rear. This seemed to be the case for the family on the pond, as the parent in the lead was the larger of the two—it made sense, at that point, for the male goose to be considerably larger than the female. The female goose does the preponderance of incubation, leaving her less time to feed. Furthermore, her body has already suffered the impact of denuding her breast for down for the nest and of producing the eggs.

On that day in May, I had come away from the house without my camera, so I had a dilemma: if I hurried home for the camera and some food, would the goslings still be visible when I got back? I decided to risk it, and the dog and I took off at a run for home. Returning without the dog within the half hour, I was thrilled to see the goslings still on display—and they did seem to be "on display." I put cracked corn on the beach near where the goose family was swimming, and they all came out (in order) to eat—not really put off by my clicking noises and incremental moves closer to them. Whether they had seen more of me at the pond in the past few weeks than I had of them, or because of the offering of food, or for whatever other reason, the parental geese seemed not too worried by me. In the weeks and months (in fact years) that followed my introduction to the family of geese, my presence was generally accepted. I was hissed back away from the goslings only very rarely, and I was never chased away—as I saw them chase other humans, other geese, and, especially, dogs.

Joe Van Wormer gives the period from nesting through incubation and the fledgling period as one hundred days.[2] However, since the period of incubation is twenty-eight days—the length of the lunar cycle—I think this estimation might not be generous enough. The geese on Bicentennial Pond were not ready for flight until late July or even early August, a length of time closer to 120 days. That is one-third of the year. Geese mate for life, usually in their third year, and will produce a clutch of goslings every year for six or seven years. Thus about one-third of their lives is spent being parents; about one-sixth of their lives, actively nurturing. And every year they start over again, facing the same long process of preparing the goslings for flight.

"Flying is the single-most strenuous activity that animals perform. A lot of goosepower is necessary to sweep those broad, fan-like wings through the air as the Canada goose strives to gain altitude."

"A big pectoral muscle (*pectoralis*) forces the wing downward; a weaker pectoral muscle (*supracoracoideus*) powers the upstroke."[3]

Geese can swim and walk within a day of hatching, but are able to fly only after considerable growth. The months on the water and in the grass are spent keeping safe, learning the habits of geese, and growing the muscles and feathers for flight. So perhaps, at least in the case of *Branta canadensis*, flight is as essential an aspect of their being as humans have made it out to be.

> "Birds that fly allocate an enormous percentage of their body resources to the flight muscles."

> "Unlike mammals, birds are equipped with a series of internal *air sacs* connected to the lungs. These air sacs can occupy up to 20 percent of the body cavity, including some of the space within large, hollow bones."

> "In comparison to animals of similar size, birds have hearts that are larger than all other vertebrates and that can be double the size of mammalian hearts."[4]

At the time of their first movements, goslings weigh about four ounces. At the end of the second week of life, each gosling will weigh approximately one pound. After six weeks, the young bird weighs five or six pounds and can run around flapping its wings. At eight weeks, each gosling will weigh nearly twenty-four times its birth weight. (As Van Wormer indicates: "At this same rate of growth, a human baby weighing 7 pounds at birth would weigh 168 pounds at eight weeks."[5]) Thus, the impact upon the pondweed and the vegetation near a pond during these weeks of growth is considerable.

> "Although feathers have many advantages, they are not perfect as a permanent body covering. The rigors of life can damage and batter feathers. Worn feathers have a reduced capacity to insulate and support birds in flight. Consequently, birds periodically replace their feathers through the process called *molt.*"

"Most North American birds replace all their feathers during a complete molt in late summer or early fall. At this time food is still plentiful, breeding is finished, and migration has not yet begun."[6]

At the same time that the young geese are growing a complete set of feathers, the parents are undergoing molt, during which period they lose and regrow their flight feathers. The entire family is flightless together for a good part of our New England summer. If the choice of nesting site has been good—plenty of food, open areas where the family can feed and keep sufficient lookout, enough water to escape predators attacking from the ground, deep enough water to discourage attacks by snapping turtles and fish, some shelter from the elements—then the goose family swims and eats its way through the soft days of May and June and the heat of July. What was apparent about Bicentennial Pond in March, when the goose pair arrived, were all of the pond's positive attributes.

The usurpation of the pond by the Parks and Recreation Department, and by the local residents who use the pond for fishing, swimming, picnicking, and finally summer camp, begins in late May, when the grassy slope becomes the background for a series of elementary school field days. Then, on Memorial Day, the pond opens for swimming on weekends, and after the school year ends the pond is in service as the town swimming area from early in the morning (lessons) until dusk (family picnics). The pond is not the idyll it had appeared to be for a goose family. I knew that the staff of the Parks Department would not want geese anywhere near the beach. I feared that the ropes and buoys they put out to mark the various swimming areas would confound the geese, and perhaps entangle them. I dreaded the incursion, at various times, of hundreds of children whose curiosity and humanness might lead them to capture, handle, manhandle, throw things at, or do violence to the young geese—who could not really escape them.

Beginning with the second week of their life on the pond, I fed the geese away from the beach, away from the playground. I was feeding them near some of the prime fishing spots, but the fishermen didn't complain. At least, not to me. When summer arrived, I wrote a letter to the Parks Department and to the Advisory Committee, hoping to give them enough information to pass along to the lifeguards, and perhaps to place in print somewhere, to keep people and geese in separate spheres, even within the same watery area. I included the information I had downloaded from the Internet that goose poop, while gross in appearance, does not have human pathogens and did not have to be the subject of abject horror.[7] In this project I was particularly lucky, because my son was a lifeguard. Poor boy—now added to his duties as swimming instructor, lifeguard, trash collector, rule enforcer, and object of admiration, he had: Instruction in "proper behavior toward young geese with whom you share the pond." There were some incidents of chasing, but neither geese nor humans were harmed that summer.

The goslings acquired tail feathers, tail coverts, upper and lower wing coverts, then primaries and secondaries. The markings of a Canada goose became evident, although muted, in the youngsters. I called the parents Mom and Dad—not imaginative but the first thing I had thought of. Because there were four goslings, I was tempted to call them by the names of the March women, the template of the family into which I was born. However, even though it might not matter to the geese, it seemed silly to bet against the odds and presume that all four goslings were female. I settled on calling them: March, the one who was always first out of the water for food; Louisa, who had the longest neck and for weeks had little tufts of down sticking out on both sides of her head like some unfortunate hairdo; May, a smaller, more polite version of March; and Alcott, who sometimes ignored food altogether and did not put on weight at the same rate as the others. I spoke to them, as I had to SG, calling them by name. Louisa eventually responded to her name and would turn her long neck so that she appeared to be hanging on my every word.

As flight feathers along the edges of their wings appeared on parents and offspring, the geese moved further and further from the pond while feeding, wandering up the hillside toward the play equipment. I tried to discourage them from this behavior, walking over and scooping air toward them with my arms extended toward the ground. They ignored me. Eventually I understood the purpose of their excursions. The hill was the training ground for flying. Mom and Dad showed their progeny how to run down the hill with wings extended and step off into the air. Eventually, each of the young geese could "fly" from the hillside into the pond, or at least drift in the air for a while before landing in the water. Then they began making longer flights, always over water so that when they lost their concentration or control, they would come splashing down into a familiar environment.

"Canada geese generally fly at altitudes from 750–3500 feet above the ground. Their flight speed is harder to measure, but is generally thought to be about 25–35 miles per hour."[8]

What an act of trust. Stepping off into an entirely different medium. In one moment to grasp the promise on which your whole life, thus far, has focused. And it was not as if they had been watching their parents fly for all those months. Okay, you can call it instinct and say that it is not as if young geese have any choice or intention in the matter, but I was there and watched them on those early flights. They came into something when they flew. I had watched my own children let go of the coffee table or the chair seat and take those first few steps, and had seen the surprise and delight (and ostentation, in the case of my daughter) in their eyes. Yet, to walk upright, even though it is what is said to have made us human in the first place, does not seem to me to be as much an investiture as a bird taking flight for the first time. Crawling and walking both take place with parts of the body firmly on the ground. Flight is a world apart, and the geese seem to realize this.

Flight is essential as a means of escape from predators. In addition, flight is community and family. Parents teach the young to fly and take them on their first flight away from the pond on which they were born and raised. Studies indicate that the migratory patterns of geese are hardwired into their circuitry: geese taken from their normal range and released will still fly until they end up where they belong. Of course, we have no way of knowing how this works—do they know the patterns of the stars, the changes in the climate; are certain smells and sights so familiar as to act as magnets; are they attuned to the earth's magnetism, or to the draw of kinship?

Mom and Dad raised five families on Bicentennial Pond: In 1998, they had March, Louisa, May, and Alcott. Here are the others as I named them.

1999   Groucho, Harpo, Chico, Zeppo
2000   Chloe, Artemis, Jack
2001   Ann, Bob, Sydney (I had to do this, once.)

In 1999, five goslings hatched, but one disappeared during the second week. In 2000, six goslings hatched. I had to be out of town for a while in late May and early June, and when I got back there were only three young geese. In 2002, we moved from the house across the street from Schoolhouse Brook Park and Bicentennial Pond. With all that there was to do for the move, I never got around to naming the three babies of that season, although I continued to feed them. In May of 2003, I drove to Bicentennial after my last visit to the campus for the semester—I am still teaching where we used to live, although I drive fifty miles to do it. No Mom and Dad, no babies on the pond on May 27. I doubt whether my absence was enough to deter Mom and Dad from nesting on the pond, but it is possible that the Parks and Recreation people used my moving away to figure out how to permanently discourage the geese from making the pond their home. I did not ask. Mom and Dad may simply have retired from the difficult work of rearing families and teaching them to fly.

For as long as I can remember I have dreamt of flying—dreamt both in the sense of a constant longing and in the sense of a nighttime's occupation. I waited for Peter Pan, seeing lights for my escape right out my window (lights, I would later discover, on the water tower). For years I swam and floated to experience the weightlessness, the freedom from gravity and gravitas I imagined were the boon of flight.

sg and I were both grounded. When I went to Hungerford I saw him amid the other flightless birds: the injured geese and sea gulls, the peacock and peahen. I had prayed for his life and his safety, but it was always difficult to see him in that diminished company. This may have been the source of the idea to tell his story: the need for others to know how brave he had been. He continued to take me on walks, still he was not any more domesticated than he had been. Even Joe commented that he was reserved. He did not eat from anyone's hand, did not come when called. He did not waddle over at the sound of my voice, although there were times I wished he had. I consoled myself with the thought that if he didn't seem elated when I was there, perhaps he didn't experience my absence, either. If he didn't remember his own days of flight, perhaps he didn't experience anything like despair when the crows drifted over his head.

One May—more than a decade before I watched Mom and Dad teach that first family to fly—I had been visiting the bird refuge on Plum Island, Massachusetts, and photographing Canada geese, who seemed to pose for their portraits. That night I dreamt I was flying, that my own body was lifted off the earth and sped above the sand and the waves. I inhabited a Chagall painting, but the landscape was the New England shore. My heart felt near bursting. Yet at the height of my exhilaration, I knew that flying meant leaving my children below, on the sand where they lay sleeping.

Going out and coming back. Flying and settling back down to earth. Caring and letting go. These were the currents of my life with the birds. I might have understood them anyway, in my human life, but it seems that it has taken the lives of geese to make the message a part of my musculature and my blood, my dreaming and waking lives.

Geese, Geese, Geese, Geese, Geese

Through millions of years, the geese have watched as bodies of water changed shape and disappeared, as grasslands expanded across continents, then burned away or were plowed under. Through all of this the geese have survived as species, and as metaphor.

Although Mom and Dad raised four goslings and taught them to fly during a recreational season at Bicentennial Pond, the head of the Parks Department had let me know that few members of the department or the community wished to continue sharing the space with the Canada geese. The next spring they put up netting between the beach and the pond to discourage the geese from coming up onto the beach and the lawn above. Their intention was to discourage the geese from living on Bicentennial Pond at all.

People do not want to live with Canada geese, and they do not feel at all restrained from expressing this preference. Few newspaper or magazine articles on Canada geese are entitled as sympathetically as the *National Geographic* article of February 1992, "Bittersweet Success," showing twenty-one Canada geese sharing a vibrantly green course with two golfers. One golfer appears to be chasing a goose away from his ball. The article mentions the mess that geese make on lawns, on golf courses and beaches, and in parks and ponds. A look at references to Canada geese in the press mostly produces a list of excoriating headlines. Wildlife biologists have taken to calling resident geese "sky carp"—referring to their plentiful numbers and implying a purely aesthetic (thus expendable) purpose. Growing numbers of wildlife experts and everyday people are raising voices of alarm in response to a Canada goose "problem": there are too many geese living in the "wrong" places.

What has changed? The natural world that nurtures Canada geese has changed. However, this time it is not the action of glaciers that has changed the surface of the earth; rather, the difference is a result of the changes we, the human population, have made to bodies of water and expanses of grass. Humankind changes the face of the earth according to its own needs and desires, and our imprint is everywhere. The geese evolved through the millions of years the planet was forming, and the geese, or at least a particular subspecies, have evolved again—and that physical change influences the way we see geese in the landscape. Our animal coinhabitants seem less magical, and we have control of the shared environment. This is not a movement away from a metaphorical way of seeing geese, it is only a way of seeing predicated on different metaphors. Furthermore, at this point in our joint history, the metaphor that shapes the way we see the geese and places them within the manhandled landscape has a greater capacity to determine how they live and whether they shall live at all.

The plentiful numbers of Canada geese who do not migrate but burden one particular locale with the impact of their livelihood is a fairly recent phenomenon. Even a decade ago, in the early 1990s, there was little in the popular press or in wildlife publications about an abundance of Canada geese. People still looked to the sky in awe as the V-shaped formations passed overhead, their long lines breaking up and reforming in a visual confirmation of the power of the messages encoded in their DNA.

However, there have always been Canada geese without that particular genius for migration. The several subspecies of *Branta canadensis* are more or less distinguished by their geographical range, as well as certain physical characteristics that have evolved within the geographic segregation. Among these subspecies is, or was, *Branta canadensis maxima*. Due to its larger size, the *maxima* did not fly the distances covered by the Atlantic, Todd's, Ross, or Brant subspecies. John James Audubon, writing in his *Ornithological Biography* Volume III about the water birds of the early nineteenth-century American Midwest, mentions a Canada goose who, as he says, "remains with us to breed" while the rest flew to the cold, unpopulated reaches of Canada to nest.[1] Flocks of resident geese were well established at the beginning of the nineteenth century, from western Ohio through southern Illinois, west across the plains of Nebraska and north through the Dakotas. Two hundred years later, human history has replaced prairies and forests with grasslands and fields of corn and wheat. Swamps, wide rivers, and large lakes have been replaced by smaller bodies of water, more accommodating to certain aspects of the goose lifestyle.

The resident flocks of the past were composed primarily of giant Canada geese, who are from one quarter to one third larger in body size than the Atlantic Canada goose (the geese who traditionally migrate through New England). The wingspread of the *maxima* may be in excess of six feet. However striking this may be to behold, large size in wild creatures has historically made them more vulnerable to the depredations of the human species. Large size usually indicates slower movements, which makes these species easier to hunt. Larger animals need more food and often slightly larger nesting areas, leaving them more susceptible to habitat destruction.

Flocks of resident geese were nondomesticated farm animals whose produce was harvested. In the nineteenth and early twentieth centuries, people took the feathers and down from their nests for making pillows, comforters, and insulated winter clothing—thus endangering the survival of the eggs and chicks who relied upon the down's insulation. Also, the eggs themselves were taken. Eventually nesting sites were destroyed to create farmland and real estate for development. The wetlands, ponds, and lakes that sustained the geese were drained, diverted, and filled in. Finally all that was left were the flocks that farmers kept for meat and feathers and to use as decoys to attract migratory geese into gun range. When the practice of using resident geese to attract migrating birds (which made hunting as easy as catching fish in a barrel) was prohibited in 1935, wild strains of resident Canada geese were considered extinct.

Then, in 1962, Harold Hanson of the Illinois Natural History Survey found a small flock of resident giant Canada geese in Rochester, Minnesota. Other birders followed Hanson's lead and soon several small flocks had been located in the north-central area of the country. In 1965, Hanson published his book *The Giant Canada Goose*, describing the plight of this species and of resident flocks in general.[2] In the wake of this book there was widespread enthusiasm for re-establishing flocks of resident Canada geese, and an enormous effort toward species restoration got under way.

Although these resident flocks were, at least by the beginning of the twentieth century, native only to the Midwest, resident flocks were established in the eastern states, also. Geese of breeding age were transported to wildlife refuges throughout the midwestern and eastern states where optimal living conditions and protection from hunting guaranteed several seasons of successful reproduction. Wildlife biologists even worked out methods for improving the security of nesting sites: for instance, wash tubs were set up on raised platforms in the water, so that breeding geese had nothing to fear from the natural predators that thin the ranks of goslings.

The program was successful, and flocks of resident Canada geese took hold in wildlife refuges where there was plentiful water, grass, and seed from wild rice and nearby fields, and the size of predator populations was regulated. However, the animals fled the zoo. The geese adapted to the land and water outside the refuges, to the other managed environments that humans create—golf courses, executive parks, municipal recreation centers, reservoirs, airport runway strips, and suburban developments. These are places humans had not intended to share with wildlife. The metaphoric birds went to live in a real world.

The geese on Bicentennial Pond are detrimental in the eyes of the town employees who supervise the park. The people who come to swim and even the fishermen do not like the goose poop on the beach and grassy verge. The panicky parents do not like the geese swimming through the area marked by buoys as human space, or wandering up toward the playground to eat the grass. The geese have not bitten or attacked the children, even the ones who have attacked them. Even if the geese do not pose a health threat, they are not good for the aesthetics of the town pond, as most people see it.

Still, the geese are rather good at adapting to living with humans. They seem to be able to avoid becoming entangled in the line that the fishermen leave everywhere around the pond. They seem not to have been poisoned by eating the cigarette butts that mark all the good fishing spots. They have learned how to swim over the buoys and to walk around the fenced-in area.

The presence of geese on Bicentennial Pond year after year is a belated result of the recovery program that took place on nearby wildlife refuges. sg's National Wildlife tracking band indicates that he is a resident goose. He was banded somewhere in Willington, the town just to the north of Storrs. This part of Connecticut is rural—even though it is bisected by Route 84, the direct route from New York City to Boston. On higher ground than Storrs, Willington has not been a farming community, and its craze of roads track through evergreen forests, not mixed growth. There are far more small bodies of water there and a few larger ones— like the millpond where local teenagers like to swim after dark. So, sg began life on one of these ponds and had flown fewer than ten miles when that part of his life abruptly ended, and he found himself a goose living not with other geese, but with humans.

Mom and Dad, and all of their young, are also resident geese. I know this not by their bands, but by virtue of their breeding on this pond. They are not geese of the Atlantic Flyway, moving back and forth from north to south, to breed one place and winter-over in another. They are the offspring of geese who have learned to live in one climate zone and to make the best of it.

It is possible to track through time the numbers of geese, or other birds, who are winter residents to a particular place by study-ing the results of the Christmas Bird Count. The Christmas Bird Count is one of the established points of reference for the study of bird populations in the United States. It is sponsored by the National Audubon Society and conducted by birding societies in every corner of the country. Much of the fieldwork in the study of bird populations is performed by volunteers, by "birders." In fact, the study of wild bird populations is made unique among other ecological studies by the high level of involvement of volunteers from all walks of life, of all ages, who dedicate so much time and energy to recording the lives of birds. Variations in numbers, in habitats, in habits; examples of interbreeding, species eradication, and revival—these are noted and reported, both in the United States and internationally, by amateur birders, who take very seriously their responsibility for the present health and the future survival of the birds of the world.

The Christmas counts tally the number of individuals of each registered species seen on a specific day at or around the winter solstice. Each local ornithological society is responsible for an area of a state, and divides that area into manageable routes for a carload of birders to traverse from sunrise to sunset—not that long a period of time so close to the shortest day of the year. These bird counts were begun in December 1900, and some ornithological societies—Greater Boston, for instance—have participated in every count, providing invaluable statistics on local species throughout the twentieth century.

There are always a few errant birds, confused souls who are off their beaten track, and we celebrate them. Still, most of the birds counted at Christmastime can be ticked off on preprinted lists of species. Most of these birds are residents of the area—birds so acclimated as to be comfortable at home even at the darkest point of winter. In New England, possibly more so than in any other part of this country, there has always been a certain honor to being a year-round resident, an even greater one in being a "native." And as much as we enjoy the return of the warblers to Connecticut, there is a lot to be said for those toughened species who hang out here all year. The Christmas Bird Count tells us how these natives are doing and measures the ecological health of an area, in comparison with past counts.

The statistics of the Christmas bird counts, which are available online through the Cornell Lab of Ornithology,[3] provide a way to chart the numbers of Canada geese who have wintered over in different parts of the country over the past one hundred years. In

Kalamazoo, Michigan—not that far from Rochester, Minnesota, where resident giant Canada geese were (re)discovered—there have been Christmas counts since 1908, although not all the numbers are available at the Cornell site. In 1966 there were two Canada geese; in 1973, eleven. But in 1974 there were seventy-eight, and then the numbers start climbing dramatically. In 1980 there were 527 Canada geese; in 1990, 2,404; in 1997, 3,634. These numbers are in part a measure of the success of the U.S. Fish and Wildlife's program to insure the continued existence of resident Canada geese in the United States.

The Christmas Count centered in Storrs, Connecticut (but encompassing most of northeastern Connecticut) was started in 1957. No Canada geese were recorded until 1968, when one was seen. Then nothing until 1975, when there were eighty-five. In 1979 there were 484; in 1989, 1,187; in 1997, 1,289; in 1999, 5,063. These numbers attest to the success of a species management program and, seemingly, the success of one species, *Branta canadensis*.

The efforts made to support nesting Canada geese were aided, indirectly, by the coincidental enactment of wetlands conservation laws and, more recently, by a string of mild winters and springs in the last decades of the twentieth century, which reduced the numbers of geese who died during the most difficult period of their annual survival. When the number of geese increased to the point where they left the refuges, they tended to move on to the places that suited their need for grain or grass and water: the aforementioned golf courses, parks, and industrial and college campuses. And recently these landscape features have increased. The last decades of the twentieth century were marked by rapid, overreaching development: rural woodlands, of little appeal to geese, quickly became landscaped into manicured greens with picturesque ponds—a resident goose's favorite homestead.

What happened was that two ill-conceived incursions by humankind radically changed the environment and changed the living habits of the geese themselves, thus disrupting the patterns of the natural world and allowing for the establishment of a (webbed) foothold into our domain. Turnabout being fair play, resident Canada geese became nuisance intruders in human existence—or at least that is how many people see them.

While the statistics on Canada geese populations might be alarming, there are a few qualifiers that ought to be kept in mind, but rarely are. For one thing these statistics are not highly scientific: the Cornell site clearly states that the Christmas Bird Count results must not be used for scientific study without verification. The numbers simply map a trend. Within the rising curve are years of downward movement: in 1986 there were 3,356 geese in Storrs at the winter count; in 1990, 773. In 1991 the numbers were back up to 2,809, but in 1997 there were fewer than half that many. The Kalamazoo numbers also fluctuate. Those who use the numbers to frighten human residents rarely concede that for wildlife, sustained growth is impossible. There are biological and other "environmental" curbs on species population. One really bad winter followed by a cold wet spring might have as devastating an impact on the geese in New England as these same conditions had on the Puritan settlers in the Massachusetts Bay Colony.

There is a good deal of discussion about how to "manage" these resident geese populations—"manage" being a euphemism, at this point, for killing them. Suburbanites walk around ponds in the spring shaking the eggs in the nests so that no chicks will hatch. This has proved an ineffective method of birth control, because quite often the female realizes that the eggs are dead and lays another clutch. In 1996, 251 Canada geese residing in Clarkstown, New York, were caught in nets, taken away, and gassed—after a health scare that was almost immediately exposed as unwarranted. The plan had been to kill about one thousand geese. In 2000, in response to the emotional levels at U.S. Fish and Wildlife Service hearings about "the Canada geese problem," the Coalition to Prevent the Destruction of Canada Geese distributed a letter for interested people to copy and send to U.S. Fish and Wildlife. The letter spoke to proposed changes in policy that would lead to "massive exterminations" and offered "Alternative G"—"Humane, Non-lethal Integrated Management Strategies"—for adoption, instead.

Of course, the hunters have been called in. Organizations of waterfowl hunters helped in the recovery program, anxious to have a favorite prey restored to good health and good numbers. By the time the geese were established enough for hunting to be allowed, the habits of the resident flocks had become apparent to all involved: these Canada geese do not fly very much or very far. For hunters to go after them would mean a return to the early 1900s, before regulations, when hunters sat by the sides of lakes and shot at anything that flew by—leaving wounded birds dying and carcasses rotting in the water and the tall grass. Leaving lead shot behind to poison future generations of wild birds. Some hunters have evolved to the point where they do not see this type of activity as sport. Furthermore, they do not want to become—as one particularly eloquent hunter put it in *Field and Stream*—the "Orkin man."[4] They don't need to be cleaning up for golfers and people with manicured lawns. A number of states, including Connecticut, have shifted their hunting season to try to ensure that only resident geese will be "bagged." But this hunting has had little effect on the population numbers—a fact that might eventually lead to some conclusions about the intelligence and adaptability of geese as compared to human hunters and policy-makers.

Allowing any hunting of Canada geese at all makes certain that some migratory birds will be killed, which poses another, more serious problem. There are still Canada geese migrating up and down the Atlantic Flyway. The geese that fly through Connecticut are *Branta canadensis canadensis*, who breed in Labrador and Newfoundland and are identified as the North Atlantic population. The mid-Atlantic population, *Branta canadensis interior*, breed on the northern Ungava Peninsula, which forms the eastern side of Hudson's Bay. Although in the 1960s and '70s the numbers of Canada geese in the Atlantic Flyway fall flight were increasing, there was a decline by at least 25 percent in the late 1980s. Between 1988 and 1996, one monitored group in the mid-Atlantic population decreased by 75 percent. Hunting of migratory geese during this period was not the only reason for the decline. There were some habitat changes in the breeding areas—some loss of habitat to human need for electricity—and there was a several-year period of bad weather for breeding geese.

By 1995, the number of breeding pairs on the Ungava Peninsula had declined from 130,000 (in 1988) to 29,000. By 1996 this number had rebounded to 46,000 primarily due to hunting bans and the curtailing of subsistence hunting by the Inuit and Cree peoples. However, the spring of 1996 was a poor year for goslings—it was cold, and many froze to death in the nest—so there were worries about the health of this population in coming years, when the few goslings who survived would be breeding. The goal of the wildlife biologists who form the American-Canadian waterfowl management group is to restore this population to 150,000 breeding pairs.[5]

Howard Norman put together a collection of Inuit tales entitled *The Girl Who Dreamed Only Geese and Other Tales of the Far North*. The title story begins with a problem. The parents of the girl, who have been responsible for dreaming only about geese and thus ensuring that there are geese to supply the people with food and warmth, are quitting.

> This disturbed everyone in the village. "It's a great privilege to dream geese," a man said to her parents. "Besides, you know full well that if you don't dream about them, the geese will be insulted and might not fly north to our marshes."
>
> "We no longer care," the girl's father said.
>
> "Geese chased by foxes. Geese squabbling. Geese shedding their feathers. Geese laying eggs. Geese honking in the sky. Geese, geese, geese, geese, geese," the girl's mother said. "We are sick and tired of doing the work of geese-dreaming!"[6]

Apparently not only contemporary suburbanites get tired of geese. The parents hand off their responsibility to their daughter. This works for three years, until the daughter's powers are interfered with by a shaman, and the village is without geese. The girl is banished; the eldest woman in the village dies. After the series of adventures necessary for the rescue of the girl, she is returned to the village, the shaman is ousted, and she dreams of geese.

> Late into morning the moon could still be seen in the sky. Geese poured down from the moon, all morning, all day. All day geese arrived to the marshes. . . . Life was familiar again. From that day forward, the girl dreamed geese very often. And dreamed only geese, nothing else.

Geese chased by foxes. Geese squabbling. Geese honking. Geese flying north. Geese flying south. The girl lived to be very, very old, she
who did the geese-dreaming work in her village, and she was greatly
respected.

Here the story ends.[7]

The girl must live with geese inside her head, in order for the
people to have geese in the marsh. The metaphoric geese and the
real geese are the same, and both bring long life.

By contrast, contemporary human response to the changes in
Canada geese populations in the Atlantic Flyway seems bipolar,
but both extremes are ultimately based upon an aesthetic or emotional response to certain habits of certain geese. On the one hand
are the efforts to increase the number of migratory geese who
breed in the northernmost reaches of the continent and fly thou-
sands of miles across desolate lands, open water, and the hostile
territory of human development to winter in the more temperate
climates of the Chesapeake Bay and the Carolinas. These geese are
described as "the true 'wild geese' of poetry, song, and folklore."[8]
To put the phrase in quotation marks is to acknowledge that it is
a label, a construct created out of our need for the "other." At the
same time, much of the human population of the United States—
at the moment supported by the U.S. Fish and Wildlife Service—
wants to diminish the number of resident geese who breed in
suburban ponds and wildlife refuges and fly ten or twelve miles
to feast on suburban lawns, farmers' fields, and grains put out
for them by humans of varying intentions—leaving their mess of
feathers and slimy excrement on human territory. Although these
geese are not domesticated, they have accommodated themselves
to the human domestication of the landscape. Thus they seem
not to be protected by the designation "wild." The literature of

the goose "problem" establishes two vocabularies: the residents are "sky carp," they are "over-familiar," "big honkers" who are "pests"—only the most forgiving of these writers acknowledge that they are "adaptable," "smart," and "resilient." The migratory birds are "thrilling," "one of the greatest birds in the world," "silhouettes against the moon," and "marathoners."

In practice, the designation "wild" may be used just as easily to place animals in gas chambers and traps and in the sights of rifles. It has been proposed that Wildlife Services be called upon to "manage" the goose "problem." Wildlife Services is the government agency formally known as Animal Damage Control. As such they were responsible for instituting programs to annihilate the wild dog of the West, the coyote. The reprehensible program of killing carried out under their auspices is detailed in Hope Ryden's *God's Dog*.[9] Ryden also delineates the lies and campaigns of disinformation used to create a vision of coyotes as having an appreciable economic impact on the sheep and cattle industries of the West. This vision, along with the cultural myth that these industries are "good," made it possible to promulgate a portrait of a "bad" animal.

So many people are angry and frightened when they look at Canada geese in the parks, on the golf courses, at the airports. But when we look at resident geese, aren't we looking into a mirror? These geese are an adaptable population with few natural limits on population growth. They are creatures whose existence seems to use up the landscape—although at least the geese do sometimes eat the leftover corn, leaving produce for other members of their own species and for other inhabitants of their ecological niche. The geese leave a great deal of noticeable waste on their environment, in the form of shed feathers and excrement. However, again, this differs from human waste, since what geese leave behind is biodegradable and nonpathogenic: not cigarette butts, soda cans, fast-food Styrofoam containers and waxed-paper wrappers, discarded metal appliances, and the fumes and other detritus from automobiles. And they are not removing native habitats or filling the earth with poisons whose murderous reach stretches far into the future.

We do not like other nondomesticated species to succeed. The cockroaches and the coyotes threaten us. We like to exercise our human imperatives by clearing the sky of birds who fly over in too great numbers.

When humankind needlessly and heedlessly slaughtered the passenger pigeon into extinction, during the last century, we lost a particular species of bird, and a host of possibilities. The passenger pigeon was, until settlers with guns put them in their sights, a very successful species. Too late we realize that no one ever accounted for their evolutionary success within their specific environment. What might we have learned from their example about the health and welfare of the planet and its inhabitants? What a wondrous metaphor for the bounty of our earth, our home, was a species of bird that, from reports that have come down to us, regularly darkened the sky with their numbers? What awe might that inspire in those of us still capable of feeling awe, still burdened with a sense of wonder?

Instead of trying to read that "wild poem" in the sky, too often our reading of Canada geese is colored by portrayals of the geese as unhealthy, of goose populations as menacing hordes who would make "normal"—that is, suburban—life impossible. A *Boston Globe* reviewer of Anne Matthews's book *Wild Nights: Nature Returns to the City* compares the Canada geese of today with those John Muir described: "Unapproachable Canada geese? The ubiquitous nuisance birds that take over suburban lawns, refuse to be shooed away, and mob hapless toddlers whose bread crumb bags are empty?"[10] Which vision shall we let guide the environmental practices and the everyday actions that will shape the future of the birds? Various Fish and Wildlife releases pit the demands of resident geese against the needs of migratory geese, almost ensuring the devaluation of this subspecies of Canada geese, while neglecting to mention the greater impact humans have had on the environment, and thus on both populations.

It is hard for me to shape these sentences that tell of wiping populations of animals from the landscape, from the face of our common home on earth. Their pain (in which I believe) and their losses are enough to darken the space before my eyes, but I am also burdened by my need for accuracy. What adjectives should I use to describe using cannons to drop nets on flocks of geese, then hauling them into a truck—mangling wings and necks, distressing them, suffocating them—to take them to the gas chamber? Can I look to the language with which Hope Ryden describes the wholesale poisoning of coyotes in such a way as to give them excruciatingly painful deaths? We tend to call such actions inhumane, but it is all too clear that humanity will treat its own species, as well as the other residents of the planet, in this manner. So many of the adjectives for this behavior, which ought to be unspeakable by reason of not being done anymore, establish a hierarchy of kindness through which we travel from lower beasts to "less civilized" mankind to the current crop. Yet, I see no such progression toward kindness, toward treating each being as if it were kin.

Behind the problem of the geese on the golf courses and on the lawns and sidewalks of executive parks—the geese in all the manicured pockets of suburbia leaving in amazing number those little piles of mucilaginous grass—is the problem of ownership. Who decides what is best for the planet, and how are those decisions made?

Canada geese were fine as long as they flew over our heads: symbols of nature's enduring patterns, vessels for our longing. We have changed the Canada goose's relationship to the environment by changing both the bird and the land it lives on. Our response to this change should not be to strip these geese of their metaphoric mantle, but to recognize our need for metaphoric geese, and to be moved by them—even the geese in the local pond. To the Canada goose, residency is a way of life. We need both science and metaphor to truly understand the situation of nonhuman creatures with whom we share this fragile earth.

At the same time, they are real geese. The geese I have lived with did not fly long distances across strange waters and lands to eat and nest and breed. They ate the turf grass on the slope to the pond; they also ate the cattails, the marsh grass, the widgeon grass, and the pondweed. They nested in the fallen oak leaves near where the swamp azaleas and the forget-me-nots bloom. They raised their young in a well-disciplined fashion in spite of the fishermen and the swimmers, the dogs who bark and the coyotes who sing at night, the snapping turtle who haunts the murky middle depths of the pond. They taught the young geese how to fly, and then they were gone by late summer, making a few reappearances in the thinning golden light of autumn. They found fields with corn the farmer has forsaken and bodies of water that do not freeze fast. They live in this world and are beings truly of the land and water, beings who shape the air. They measure time by the quality of light; seasons, by temperature and the changing of winds. They nurture the next generation, even as they somehow register their losses. Their individual lives are the result of millions of years of adaptation and repetition.

Without them, my life would be inestimably poorer—as would the emotional, imaginative, and physical lives of millions of other human beings. Still, that is not really the point. They belong to and with the elements. And the species that is tearing at the inter-relationships between elements and beings of this planet needs to desist. For a while we have been using intellect and technology, our special gifts, to figure out ways to grant special places for the life of the planet to breathe, swim, fly, and metamorphose as it has for millennia. However, the human world is no longer contained on one side of the windows of houses, factories, and cars and has infected that "other world" with agents of death that may act more quickly than life's ability to adapt. And still, we do not take the time or trouble to understand how it is we live.

The End of Gazing

I visited SG at the Hungerford Outdoor Educational Center fairly regularly, because my daughter ran and the track where her team had all the big meets was only minutes away. Since my daughter ran the thirty-two-hundred-meter race (one of the last events of a meet), I had more than enough time to drop her at the track and head over for a visit to SG. He would walk me around the yard, periodically looking over his shoulder at me, while I filled him in on what was happening at the pond. We fell easily into the relationship we had had on the pond: silent goose leading chattering woman.

SG was not the only Canada goose at Hungerford, of course. During SG's tenure there were usually six to ten Canada geese. There were always a few seagulls and mallard ducks, birds whose lives bring them into constant contact with human activity. All of these birds had been injured in some way so that they could not fly. One poor Canada goose only had one leg, so, you see, there was no way for her to launch herself into the air, even though both wings were intact. There was a domestic Muscovy duck who fearlessly and rather belligerently guarded the parking lot. There were domestic (white) geese. There were a peacock and a peahen, given to the center when their owner discovered their beauty was not as pleasing as their screams were frightening. There often was a crow, but I was never sure whether he was an inhabitant, or just someone who came by for a free meal. And, of course, there were rock doves on the roofs.

The center was a haven not only for birds. There were some sheep, a cow of Asian or Indian descent (really very friendly), and a goat. Injured, discarded, inconvenient animals. They were fed and housed. Cleaned up after. People came to tour the exhibits about animal and bird habitats; they came for programs like Farm Yard Fun and Animals Wild and Tame. None of those animals at the center was living the life the murals inside depicted, although through no fault of their own.

Human-animal cohabitation, John Berger postulates, has been corrupted by the changes in (Western) human society. When animals and mankind were companions, the wisdom that accompanied the fact that animals "were subjected *and* worshipped, bred *and* sacrificed" informed our lives together and the narratives of those lives.[1] Beginning in the eighteenth century, under the spreading cloud of industrialization, animals became machines rather than companions. By the twentieth century, for most of the Western world, animals had become raw material. The category "animal" lost its central importance, and the images of animals were co-opted into either *family*—Beatrix Potter, Disney, pets (creatures with no lives of their own)—or *spectacle*, creatures once invisible whom technology has made visible, but who are always observed.[2] The birds and animals at Hungerford illustrated this division. The murals and videos provided for education directed the visitors' responses to the injured—but familiar—creatures in the yard, with the few celebrity creatures—peacocks, Muscovy duck, "diversified" cow—treated almost as exhibits in a sideshow.

I do not fault the excellent staff at Hungerford for this state of affairs. They not only provided for the material needs of these animals, but tried to arrange for them to have something more: space to move around in, a pond for the swimmers, companionship, and no restrictions on noise making. However, to keep the visitors and financial support coming in, they had to fit their guests into the narrow confines within which the culture views them. One way for me to make sure SG was treated well was for me to keep visiting and reminding everyone that SG had a name and a story, and by doing just that I was helping to make him more an object of someone's gaze—and less a bird.

In Javanese mythology every man has a house, a woman, a horse, a dagger, and a bird. The bird is the symbol of beauty, of distraction. The intricate facts of bird flight, the aestheticism of bird song, the mysteries of migration have made birds the vessels for human envy, longing, and wonder across many cultures. In birds we find the metaphors for our highest achievements in lyric language. Berger argues that because animals are like and unlike, held distant from us by the absence of language—or the absence of our recognition of their intelligible communication—they are perceived as having secrets. Thus, animals enter the human imagination as "messengers and promises."[3] This is overwhelmingly the case when we write about birds.

Flight, song, loss, and return. As with the other subject matter for our writings of the natural world, birds are objectified in the process of being described, appreciated, conjectured upon. Inevitably it is not birds who are the subject of our song. When we write about birds, most of the time what we write about is ourselves.

To some extent, this is inevitable. There is this distance between the nature we write, read, and live within, and the mind wherein our feelings and intelligences are apprehended and put into language. We struggle with the distance between subject and word, and with how to take distance into account in our appreciations of nature and in our writing. Even before we can talk about birds as birds, not as embodiments of the mystery of flight, we have to identify the substance of the veil that must be lifted between us.

In the English language, birds and the metaphors they inspire in our response to them are prevalent in our poetry. Flight is the single metaphor for both—the apparently effortless movement that allows the human mind, as well as the substance of the bird, to leave earth and the mundane. Flight is a manifestation of physical adaptation and prowess that we envy and seek to emulate, but which will always be mysterious. The unaided flight of birds is unattainable to humankind except in dreams. The heron takes his long, slow drifting beats that barely seem to disturb the mist, that sleepy meeting place of air and water, over the morning pond. The imposing, even threatening, substance of the hawk suspends itself in a medium so thin, so insubstantial, that we are for the most part unconscious of taking it into our own bodies with a necessary constancy. The goldfinch dips in flight like a roller-coaster car suddenly discovering gravity, yet can pulsate into a frantic gyre, waiting for a place at the feeder.

For the metaphor to work, there has to be a real bird to be seen, outlined against the sky. There has to be some understanding of the mystery and promise of flight. A rhetoric of writing about the natural world might need to include the principle that the vehicle must continue to exist. Would this change the way we write? Would we write less often about the emotions associated with the birds and animals of the world and more often about their real, and often endangered, lives? For if we blink in our observations, we may perpetuate a blind spot—into which the real disappears.

John Tallmadge has written of a "disciplined subjectivity": writing that gets the facts right and expresses feelings, such as wonder and the recognition of spirit, that we expect from writing about the natural world.[4] An example might be Aldo Leopold's passage about the return of geese in March. In his knowledge of the length of time the genus *Branta* has been in flight over our earth and of the patterns of the migratory routes, Leopold displays the erudition Tallmadge puts forth as one of the dual virtues of disciplined subjectivity. However, giving value to such erudition, to the study of the received natural history of birds that often precedes fieldwork, may cast a pall over the writing. As Barbara Noske illustrates, the doctrine of human mastery over nature is an essential philosophical underpinning for experimental natural science (and its objectification of animals)—and mechanistic approaches to nature discount a living nature imbued with a directive life force or a nature coming into existence as a result of some "final cause."[5]

Leopold's essay hints at the importance of a certain species in a particular bioregion—in the relationship of geese and grain—but its primary impact is in revealing how one man was emotionally charged by the movements of the geese. He recounts the facts of the history of these migrations with such incantatory power that we are swept along into admiration of the mystery. Yet we are still a considerable distance from knowing about the lives of the birds who migrate, from an expression of their lives as subject matter. And what admiration may wash over from the mystery to the birds themselves is, at least in part, colored by self-congratulation for the human ability to quantify time, bird migration, mystery itself.

To promote erudition before (either chronologically or ontologically) the work of the imagination and the heart grants the writer-naturalist leeway to stay within the mind, to stay the Other—to continue to anthropocentrically value the ratiocination we can account for over whatever goes on in the lives of birds (and other animals). To move away from anthropocentrism is not simply a cause to be taken up in order to tell a better story. The privileging of the human perspective on the natural world, it has been argued, is a speciesism that springs from the same poisonous philosophical ground as racism.[6]

To let go of the "privileged" position of the rational mind would require something like the action advised by William Beebe, as described by Jim Papa:

> "To write honestly and with conviction . . . about the migration of birds, one should oneself have migrated." [Beebe] did not mean that one should have simply moved from one place to another, but that one should have at one time forsaken all security and safety and given oneself over completely to an inner urge which reason could not explain, a desire whose outcome couldn't be guaranteed.[7]

This kind of participatory disciplined subjectivity would seem to require that the writer-naturalist identify the essence of the bird's experience and imaginatively construct, and partake in, some comparable experience.

This is something akin to what Rachel Carson did in order to write the narrative of the sanderlings Silverbar and Blackfoot.

> Now for the first time an abiding fear entered the heart of Silverbar—the fear of all wild things for the safety of their helpless young. With quickened senses she perceived the life of the tundra—with ears sharpened to hear the screams of the jaegers harrying the shore birds on the tide flats—with eyes quickened to note the white flicker of a gyrfalcon's wing.
>
> After the fourth chick had hatched, Silverbar began to carry the shells, piece by piece, away from the nest. So countless generations of sanderlings had done before her, by their cunning outwitting the ravens and foxes. . . .

Now the sanderling mother knew by instinct that the depression in the tundra, lined with dry leaves and lichens and molded to the shape of her breast, was no longer a safe place for her young. The gleaming eyes of the fox—the soft pad, pad of his feet on the shales—the twitch of his nostrils testing the air for scent of her chicks—became for her the symbols of a thousand dangers, formless and without name.[8]

Anthropomorphism: the image of the animal with a human subjecthood—worse, with a name—has long been interdict for nature writers. Of course, there are gradations of anthropomorphism. In its purest form, there would be no vestige of animal in the image, and all that could be seen would be human life, human consciousness—perhaps dressed up as lion or bear or deer. Yet to posit a pure anthropomorphism, a pure subjectivity of writing animal lives, would seem to mean that there is also a pure objectivity, in which animals are only observed. From what we know about human consciousness, we know that this is impossible. The ways that we constitute meaning color what we say is the truth.

At any rate, nature writing about animals, in this case about birds, is always somewhere in between. It is possible that within this spectrum, within the various ways in which we talk about birds, there are differences that are more than a matter for literary (or political or philosophical) distinction. There are ways of talking about birds that make them the subjects of their own lives: both writing that takes birds as subject matter and writing using birds as metaphors. It is possible—in the observed detail, the attribution of meaning, the recognition of something beyond the meaning the human mind can affix to the natural world—to recognize the "birdness" of birds. It may even be possible to recognize the individuality of birds.

Why do this? Why even look for, hope for, this possibility? As Berger says, "Why look at animals?" In our culture, animals have been almost completely marginalized physically: into "wilderness," into zoos, into laboratories, into factory farms. When Berger looks at animals it is because he sees in the treatment and representation of animals a mirror of the appalling treatment of humanity under the culture of capitalism. He accepts that we see ourselves in animal lives—that *we* are what we talk about—because he wants us to see how we can be better human beings.[9]

However, we needn't always be talking about ourselves. In fact, there are compelling reasons to change the way we talk about birds. The birds live their lives among the destruction of the forests, the pollution of the air, the rising levels of toxicity of the land caused by pesticide use on factory farms, and the dumping of wastes created by overconsumption. If we do not find a way to talk about birds that makes them the subjects of their own lives, if we do not find a way to represent bird life as it is in the physical world, we will eventually lose the presence of birds. If they disappear from our stories, they will disappear from the landscape. That loss cannot be fathomed, as Linda Hogan reminds us:

> As we lose the animals, it is not only clear that our own health will soon follow, but some part of our inner selves knows that we are losing what brings us to love and human fullness. Our connection with them has been perhaps the closest thing we have had to a sort of grace.[10]

The interdiction against anthropomorphism in writings about animals is rooted in the idea that such transference is "unscientific." One of the results of this has been that animals have been treated—as subjects of narratives and much more—as if they had no minds at all. Yet studies, fieldwork, and narratives have all shown that animals have cognitive rationality, instrumental rationality, language, metacommunication, and a knowledge of death.[11] Even with this objective footing, there continues to be a general nervousness about one's writing being labeled anthropomorphic. Perhaps the recognition that the practice of nature writing encompasses the objectivity of science and the subjectivities of metaphysics, imagination, and truth may lead us past this point. The case against anthropomorphism should be not that animals do not have minds, lives, and subjecthood, but that the alternative to nonsubjecthood is not *human* subjecthood.

How do we tell animal stories truly, in a way that matters? Linda Vance suggests four criteria for the ethical narrative of animal life: It should be ecologically appropriate to a given time and place, be ethically appropriate in that time and place, give voice (informed by both observation and imagination) to those whose stories are being told, and make us care. "The goal is . . . to make us care about animals . . . because they are themselves."[12]

When we write about flight, song, loss, and return—when we talk about birds and when we read what others have written—we have to have a certain amount of faith. We look for the signs that the writer-naturalist has done a good job in the field. We must believe that what the writer tells us is what was seen. We need to have faith in interpretations based on work in the wild and common fields of life. We have to have faith that poetry, by which is meant any creative writing, can change the world—can change the way people see and feel and think. Because in order to participate in the earth's rescue, we will have to think and see and feel as poets—and understand a different order to the world.

Two Geese and a Duck on a Pond in Winter

The practice of going to the pond—begun in late 1996 with my ministrations to SG and renewed in 1998 when goslings were my focus—was ritual for five years. In the summer, visits to the pond had to be timed so that the dog and I did not interrupt swimming lessons, which my son taught, and did not appear as the dinner-time picnickers arrived. We found little snatches of time. In the fall, the grassy hill fell away before us, clear of human figures, and the pond sparkled in a light being cleansed of humidity. In the early morning, the heron was on the pond along with the geese and ducks—you could almost set your watch by his eight-o'clock departure. The geese on the pond those autumn mornings were forming the communities they would maintain until spring. Mom and Dad and the goslings, now fairly grown, swam in and out of the flock. Late in the fall of 1998, after I watched the goslings learn to fly, and had seen the pond emptied of all geese in the afternoons, I came to realize that there were hangers-on at the pond: birds there when they should not have been; birds in circumstances like SG's. And I began to think of my daily visits to the pond as a way to look in on two geese and a duck who seemed to be stranded there.

Before long, I knew why the duck was there, on a New England pond that was closing up for winter. Having practiced with the story of SG, I want to be sure to tell these stories more expertly. I'll tell you only what I feel sure I know, about the duck and the geese and the pond. I want to carve away all the guesses, all the little assumptions, all the thinking that is really just a way of making my mind the focus of my gaze. Such Zen-like self-consciousness and self-abnegation will be hard, but it is, I think, what really needs to be done.

The duck, a female mallard, was there because her right wing was broken. It dangled at her side when she left the water, and was not completely tucked against her side when she swam. She could not fly, thus she could not go off with the other mallards to water that would stay open all winter, where there would be some vegetation to eat to get them through.

Her wing may not have curved tight against her mottled brown body, but she swam quite well, paralleling my path along the shore. She was always first to separate herself from the group on the water and follow me over to the spot near the tall grass where I left the mounds of scratch food. In response to her speed and her independence, the lines from a television show theme song came into my mind. I called her Paladin. "Where will you roam? / Paladin, Paladin, / Far, far from home." Even in telling you this, I have slipped from the story of the duck into the story of my mind. I transported across species boundaries the associations that were the source of the name. Yet it is also the case that I cannot tell the story without the name. Perhaps there would not even be a story if I hadn't named the duck, if I hadn't been the kind of person who walks over to a pond nearly every day to feed the birds. Those who give names to the birds single themselves out, leave themselves open to the work of the narrator. This story, like so many stories about animals, is a story of singularities, of differences.

Looking at Paladin and her broken wing, I saw the months stretch out in front of us. I knew I would be spending time with

her for a while—until late December or January when the pond
froze over and I would be able to rescue her and take her to a rehabilitator. Although I knew why Paladin was on the pond, I cannot say what, if anything, Paladin knew about her presence there.
What I can say is that she acted as if she knew why I was there.
When I showed up, she directed her attention to me, to where I
was going as I walked the edge of the pond. She was at that scratch
feed very quickly. She seemed to get used to me and came out of
the water while I was still shaking the last few chaffy bits of kernels
out of the plastic bag and stuffing it back into the pocket of my
jacket. Although she looked at me as we did our tandem circum-
navigation of the pond, once she had food before her she rarely
gave a glance in my direction, thus signaling (as I read it) that she
understood she had nothing to fear from me.

However many birds are on the pond in late summer, they all
get used to my appearance and the appearance of food when I
am there. With each visit, more and more of them will come out
of the water closer to me. They are not without shyness, for they
still glance at me with half-raised heads—the geese especially.
They are ready to stretch out their long necks and lunge after
me hissing and nipping, if I give them cause. But I do not. I do
not try to get too close. I do not want them used to my presence
within the circle of their awareness. I want them shy of humans,
who are—almost universally—the enemy. I only want to be able
to get a little closer to them, to observe their habits with each
other. I cannot be like another goose or duck, and I cannot be a
friend. I wish I could be invisible.

Paladin's presence on the pond in winter could be explained as a
biological imperative. The presence of the geese was less compre-

hensible. One of them, Spot, had shown up in July, when Mom and Dad still had the four young ones swimming on the pond between them. The first time I saw Spot he was preening himself on a small point of land near the southern end of the pond, just beyond the little area that had become grassless from the feet of fishermen and geese—one of the places where I put down food. In the action of moistening his beak with oil and spreading it on his feathers, he left a downy, white feather affixed to his forehead. From a distance it looked like he had a white spot on his forehead. Very distinctive. And kind of silly looking.

It was unusual for a goose to show up on the pond in the middle of summer. The geese who are too young to mate are elsewhere, all together, hanging out on some larger body of water. Doing what adolescents do—but staying out of the way of the family units. Yet, here was Spot, an unattached goose, plopping himself down on a pond already inhabited by a family. On that first day I did not see Mom or Dad display any of the antagonism they had shown other intruders. Neither took off over the grass to hiss at Spot, who was only about twenty feet away. Nor did they muscle the young ones, now nearly as big as their parents, into a tighter group, but allowed them to keep feeding in their own desultory fashion.

In the days and weeks afterward, from midsummer through Labor Day (by which time the young ones were really flying) and beyond, I watched as Spot followed the goose family around from a safe distance. Mom and Dad were raising their first brood on this pond, so I had to wonder if Spot was one of last year's babies having trouble separating himself from family. It seemed unlikely. And, although I had fed the geese on the pond the previous fall, I did not remember Spot (who was unusual looking) being there. It didn't seem that he was instinctually returning to where he could get food. For whatever reasons, he came. He became the family's shadow: he swam near them and ate after they were done with the piles of cracked grain. He must not have caused any trouble; no one chased him away. (Because I know so little about what goes on in goose families, I have to state the facts by way of negatives.)

Spot was there, with the goose family, in early fall, when geese started to reassemble on the pond. To say reassemble makes it sound as if this were a plan, as if the groupings were cohesive. I do not know that either is the case. In the fall, as the sun shifts its position in the sky, when the mature geese are done molting and the young ones have learned to fly, numbers of geese come together on bodies of water that will accommodate them. The geese convene late in the afternoon, talk among themselves, and sleep on the water. Midmorning they leave to feed.

The annual ice age comes in late October and early November. The edge of the pond is brittle every morning so that the geese have to crack through it to get to the food I leave or to the grass slowly growing gray, or just to sit in the warm sun as it falls on the hillside. Beginning sometime in late September fifty or more geese will spend the night on the pond, take off together at about nine o'clock in the morning, and regroup at dusk. Under normal circumstances, they all leave one day to regroup in still greater numbers on lakes that will stay largely free from ice. But this fall of which I write—this autumn of Paladin, after the summer when Spot became not quite one of Mom and Dad's family—when the mass of geese left, there were still two geese and a duck left on the pond as winter approached.

I kept feeding them. I assumed there was also something wrong with Spot and his companion, a slight, reserved goose. The existence of these birds on the pond at this time of the year was the efficient cause of my actions, which are what I am recording. If I had learned one thing from taking care of a solitary goose, it was that a goose on a pond that is freezing over cannot leave. It is not a proper conclusion to draw that a goose will become so enamored of me or the food to want to stay when instinct and the flock tell him to leave. SG stayed because he was disabled. No geese had stayed just to visit with me.

Staying was death. What can we know of how animals perceive death—the loss of others or their own mortality? Mom and Dad lost goslings. In the spring of 2000, they started out, in early May, with five goslings. There were five downy beings swimming the length of the pond within days of being hatched. In spite of instinct and physical adaptation, in less than two weeks' time the five had become three. It is difficult not to believe that the parent geese recognized the difference between five goslings and three. They have to register these losses. We might like to believe that they do so without what we call emotion, but that is another discussion. It may be instinct that guides them away from situations where Death sits with open jaws, but it is acknowledgement that comes into play when a being who was once there, beside you in the water, is no longer.

How can we completely separate instinct from perception? On one spring day after the two goslings disappeared, there was another pair of Canada geese on the pond, and Mom and Dad did not like that at all. Mom and Dad took turns making their water-skimming lunges at the intruders—body flattened out, neck elongated, head just inches above the water—hissing stridently. While one of the pair sent this "keep away" message to the intruders, the other held to one place in the water, letting the goslings cluster around. Then, suddenly, the response to the intruders went to a different level. There was a hoarse, parental vocalization, and all three goslings dove into the water. I was so astonished that I did not time their disappearance, but thinking back to the occurrence I would guess the babies were underwater for about five seconds. Then they bobbed back up, still close to the safe zone their parents defined. This underwater escape occurred several more times. Eventually one of the goslings came up about two feet away from his siblings and had to paddle with his little body thrust forward to get back to where he belonged.

Questions spring to mind as fast as that little guy swam. Why did Mom or Dad goose choose a "danger" response to two other members of the same species? What, if anything, changed to make Mom and Dad shift from the standard response towards an intruder—lunging and hissing—to this underwater alternative? What is the purpose of such a tactic? Are these responses designed to protect the goslings or the parents? Are the babies out of danger because they are invisible? Is the underwater tactic used in response only to threatening *birds*, who presumably cannot attack the young ones underwater?

This last question made me wonder whether Mom and Dad had used this tactic recently against another source of danger (a dog? a snapping turtle?), and it hadn't worked, resulting in the deaths of two of their offspring. But these are precisely the kinds of questions I have been trying not to ask, because I cannot answer them without reaching levels of assumption and inference I hope to avoid. What I observed was that these Canada geese parents recognized danger—even from a source that a somewhat informed, human bystander did not see as threatening—and acted upon that recognition. Furthermore, by displaying two different actions in response to, presumably, the same danger, the geese represented themselves as having a choice of instincts, a choice of responses. They tried both of them. The other pair of Canada geese swam away. The next day the intruders were not at the pond, and the three surviving goslings were still there, swimming between their parents.

Our current behavioral perspective on these kinds of responses by birds to habitat change is to say that they are instinctual. We say that instinct provides them with an escape plan, without their actually knowing from what they are escaping. Somehow they know when their habitat is becoming uninhabitable, and they respond to that situation. The ice is coming; time to move on. Perhaps we may make this distinction: that geese "recognize" danger, but do not "know" death. This is to say that the birds do not "know" death as we do. However, does that mean that they do not choose to flee from death, but are somehow programmed away from the jaws that bite, the claws that catch?

My knowledge of Canada geese is based primarily upon my observations of their behavior. It is not a very rigorous study. Yet, I have been with them in their environment. I have watched them leading their own lives, not performing some task that I felt would determine some aspect of their intelligence, or other inner life. I think they may very well know where and what death is. We extol the role of instinct in animal lives, and in some instances in human lives, and its greatest role is to make us living beings turn away from death. Instinct would seem to make us "choose" life, even though an instinctual action belies choice as its cause. But that may not always be the case. Might it be that birds do not always "choose" life, safety, the path away? This question brings me to the consideration of the third bird on the pond.

Spot's companion was a goose who was "failing to thrive," to use the terminology of a nurturer. When I brought food for Paladin and Spot, this goose didn't even swim over to shore. Spot would come for the food, eat, and then swim back out to his companion. Because this "failing" goose was slight, I came to identify him with one of Mom and Dad's young offspring. In fact, I was convinced, on very little objective evidence, that this goose was Alcott. Alcott had been the one who just did not seem interested. He ate sparingly. Nibbling a few kernels, then turning to go back for a drink of water, or to groom himself. He wandered around the food pile. I encouraged him to eat, but I do not remember ever seeing Mom or Dad get on his case about nutrition. So, in my mind, the one goose from my experience who did not eat was a constant. By the simplest of logical axioms, the goose on the pond in winter who was failing to thrive was, therefore, the goose I had named Alcott.

What this goose was doing, on the small New England pond heading into winter, was dying. Alcott, as I called him, did not fly off during the day to get food. He did not, to the best of my knowledge, eat the food I brought. It is possible that he only came to the food after I left the premises, but from what I saw there was little left after Paladin, Spot, and the crows—the birds who were thriving and not shy about doing it with me around—got done with it.

It takes an enormous effort to stay alive. There is the calorie intake necessary just to breathe and to keep the heart pumping, which with a bird's circulatory system is a considerable job. Also, birds produce a good deal of heat, so those fires must be stoked. The muscles must be provided for, because without them there is no flight, and without flight there is no food and no escape from predators. There is the activity of finding food, in the winter especially arduous, and there is activity involved in maintenance. A water bird must not only preen its feathers daily for flight, but must oil them in order to stay waterproofed and afloat and warm.

The goose who was failing to thrive was not making an effort. He wasn't really doing anything that I could see. As the days and nights grew colder, I found him in the morning sitting out in the little bit of clear water in the middle of the pond. By "clear" I mean free from ice. In fact at this point in the seasons the water that is still free of ice is more opaque than the ice. It is a turgid, grayish brown. The fact that there was still clear water meant that the ice was not firm enough for me to walk on, or I might have ventured out to feed Alcott, as I had done for SG.

Death is the natural process. I say "the" because we could choose to see that it is death that begins the moment the egg cracks open and the gosling stumbles, chest first, out into the nest of pond grass, last year's dead leaves, and mother's down. Death is always where we are going. In its way it is a dance like the waltz. The partners change positions with relationship to the progress across the floor. Sometimes she has her back to the line of dance; sometimes, he. One-two-three. Life-and-death. One. Two. Three.

On Christmas Day my husband and I took the dog for a celebratory walk to the pond. We took scratch feed for the two geese and the one duck. We reached the crest of the basin within which the pond rests and looked down at what, in another season of the year, would have been the shore. Alcott lay dead and frozen. His eyes had already been harvested, by crows I presume. My husband took the carcass and wedged it into the side of the stone wall behind the bathhouse, above the pond. There the fox would have no trouble getting at it and, we hoped, would not get the idea that the pond was a source for more of the same.

Spot and Paladin were still at the pond. Spot was out on the ice, which covered the pond at this point and seemed to be fairly firm.

Paladin was down by the little open spot where the freshet comes in through the pipe, a place SG had frequented. It was time to start thinking about getting these two off the pond.

New Year's Day was quite cold and I rose early, determined to start the new year by saving a life. I left the dog at home and set out for the pond before anyone else was even dressed. I took a little food and a blanket. I could not capture both birds at once, even at one try. Getting SG off the ice had taken six people and well over an hour of negotiations. I figured if I could get Paladin by myself, then I could get the rest of the family, and perhaps a friend, to help with Spot later in the day.

Both birds were in their usual places, and I dumped the food near Paladin. She went right to it, barely looking in my direction— and barely five feet away from me. I did not want to just throw the blanket on her while she was eating: I reasoned that if I did she would never trust me, or any other human, again, and if she were going to live in captivity, this would be a disadvantage. This is, of course, my putting ideas into her head, but I offer this ratiocination here as the reason why I did not take this first, good opportunity. When she had eaten some and was walking away, I followed, gently herding her onto the ice, where I assumed that I would have the advantage over a small, web-footed, lopsided duck.

It is not as easy as it sounds to throw a blanket over a bird. One instinct that all birds I've encountered have is to escape from any force of wind coming at them, and I was not that sure of either my forcefulness or accuracy with the blanket. In order to have the blanket actually fall onto Paladin I felt I would need to be fairly close, say within three feet. Well, Paladin was having nothing to do with letting me get within blanket-throwing range. We shuffled across the pond, a two-clown parade: Paladin, slightly off-kilter due to her damaged wing, leading me, while I tried to keep my footing and to close the gap between us—holding the blanket behind my back. She kept looking over her shoulder at me. To see if I was still there? To see what I was up to? I was still there, but I never felt I had a good chance with the blanket.

Paladin led me off the ice and into the woods, and there I thought, again, that I would have an advantage. The woods are uneven and littered with dry, slightly slippery oak leaves. But, of course, Paladin could walk beneath the lowest hanging tree branches where I had to duck (if you'll excuse the expression) and worry about things snapping into my eyes.

Paladin was not taking delight in this chase. Her gait increased; her wing dragged a bit more. It seemed clear to me that she was in distress. I needed to get her in the blanket and on her way to safety before she exhausted herself or ended up with a further injury. In the woods, when I was just barely at the outside of what I judged to be my range, I threw the blanket. And missed. Not completely, but Paladin scurried out from under the edge of the blanket. Now I had a problem. Now she did not trust me, and I would never get close enough to catch her.

I returned to the house and admitted my hubris to my family. I had tried to catch Paladin by myself. There were no recriminations. My husband and two children put on enough clothing for the occasion. My son grabbed the airline carrier we had converted for bird transportation (by pulling out the cat-urine-scented pegboard floor and replacing it with straw). Someone picked up another blanket, and we headed off across the street.

By then it was midday, and there were three or four boys playing hockey on the ice. I assumed that their presence, their noise, would so alert Spot and Paladin that we would never be able to get close enough to scoop them up. The plan was still to get Paladin first. We had two blankets, and maybe we thought we could get both birds in one trip, perhaps even get both of them into the carrier, which can accommodate a large dog or two cats. We had not really thought this through to the end. But we were determined.

We formed a large circle around Paladin and carefully started pulling the circle smaller. She moved out onto the ice and closer to the hockey players. Two of the hockey players—boys in their early teens—skated near enough to ask what we were doing. We told them we were capturing injured birds to save them from freezing. We explained that we needed to form a circle around the duck to control her movements, and then get close enough to throw a blanket on her. So they skated over to join the circle, and I think they made the difference. On skates they were faster and could react more quickly to the slight changes in direction Paladin effected constantly. Their hockey sticks were like third legs, making the circle around Paladin even more restrictive. In just a few minutes I had her under the blanket, then gently enclosed, blanket and all, in my arms. I scuttled over to the waiting carrier, speaking thanks over my shoulder.

A bird has substance. Even a small bird is matter, and twigs will bend under the weight of a bird tucking in to rest there. Yet a bird is physically composed of slight, hollow bones. And much of what we take to be the substance of the bird is feathers, which are, indeed, an aspect of their physical being, but are so light that the rational mind holds them next to nothingness. One feather, held in hand, even a primary feather from a large, powerful bird—a hawk or a turkey vulture, for instance—almost fails to register with the sense of touch. I see the feather, but I barely feel it. Without that sensing of weight to back up the visual input, the visual could be an illusion. Fog, a ghost, a dream.

A bird-full of feathers, though, must have enough substance to register that it is matter. So many feathers times next to nothing. It is almost like those juvenile jokes in which something must be multiplied by zero. The result is still an armful of lightness. Truly the lightness of being. I have held songbirds in my hands many times. Early in my life I discovered that I could fold my hands around a bird—like holding a living, fluttering prayer. I wonder if the magician feels the privilege of opening hands to the flap of wings and the passage of bird-being into the air from whence it came.

A bird with something over its head is very still. That is why the falconers fashioned hoods when they harnessed the killing power of the birds of prey to humanity's wanton destructiveness. Paladin inside the blanket, inside the hold of my arms, seemed not to be there. There wasn't an alarm reaction to the darkness of the blanket world. Perhaps the blanket in some way replicates the darkness of the underwater world into which the young geese disappear for protection. We cannot know that, no matter how many experiments we run, how much time we spend at the edge of the pond. Are there tribes of humans who escape to the dark? We of the artificially lighted world—so pervasive that we now have to legislate the needed darkness—do not appreciate the dark as comfort.

Even sleep is but a preparation for death. Is that why we seem, generation by generation, to want to do away with sleep? Why we invent laborsaving devices that allow us, at every turn, to spend more of each diurnal rotation ignoring our biological responses to day, to night? Each generation gets less sleep than the preceding one. Each generation creates more-efficient methods of mass destruction, perhaps in part out of the despair created by sleeplessness, the despair born of rejecting the comfort of the dark.

Yet here I must return my narrative to the ice. Because here comes the good part. I slipped Paladin into the carrier and she resigned herself into the straw. Pleased at how well the rescue had gone with the hockey players helping, I announced we should try to get Spot at that moment, extra help and blankets at hand. Without really waiting for any response I turned and ventured back onto the ice, walking toward Spot. Spot took me out onto the ice at the middle of the pond, where I am most anxious. I was following him the way that I had followed SG across the ice. I thought, this is going to be another long, negotiated process—a dance of closeness and trust, then distance and a reminder of the unreachable expanse of ice, water, nothingness between the species.

Out in the middle of the pond, where the winter sun shone brightest—it was a beautiful day—and the blue sky stretched widest on all sides, where it seemed Spot and I stood at the middle of our universe, he turned to face me. I thought that he might come to me the way SG had come calmly to be taken. I moved the blanket from behind my back to my chest as carefully as I could. Spot looked right at me, stretched out his wings, and took off. He flew just inches over my head. I thought I saw him looking down at me, teasing me. In my heart I heard him saying, "I could always fly."

The communication could not have been more real. He could fly. He had waited until I was so close that his wing tips nearly touched my head in their downward stroke when he took off. He flew down to the end of the bit of sky above the pond, then turned and flew back above me at greater altitude, to the narrow end of the pond where the bridge is, then turned back toward me. He landed on the ice twenty or thirty feet away. I just stood there laughing and crying. My husband informs me that, quite unnecessarily, I said, "Look, Spot can fly."

I took Paladin over to our house and called the bird rehabilitator, who had been told that a handoff was imminent. The rehabilitator informed me that if, as I averred, Spot had not flown any great distance in a matter of months, he had allowed the muscles necessary for flight to atrophy. I had a slight reprieve from the loss of the routine of caring: I was to go to the pond daily and make Spot practice flying.

The last installment of the story of two geese and a duck on the pond began the next day. Spot seemed to enter into this game wholeheartedly. I would walk out to him on the ice, getting fairly close, and raise my arms in the same manner I did when "raising" pigeons from the ground. Thirty years ago a New York City friend taught me how to raise pigeons in Washington Square Park by coming up to a host of them on the ground with arms extended at one's sides, just off the body, and gently but firmly and slowly raising the arms. The pigeons take flight in an orchestrated wave of cooing and wing beating. My children, at ages seven and nine, were delighted to learn this trick when we took them to Europe—the poor children had never yet lived in much of a town, let alone a city where there were hordes of pigeons. I have a photograph of them elevating pigeons at the foot of Giotto's Bell Tower in Florence, causing an effect with the pigeons around the bell tower not unlike the up and down movements of the wooden horses around the carousel. I had to stop them when they got too excited and started running after the birds; disaster of one sort or another was imminent.

I do not know the origins of this practice. My friend was from Appalachia.

When I was encouraging Spot to practice flying, I would yell, "Fly, dammit!" Off he would go. He made a few circuits of the pond, and then landed near the food I'd left. I think he spent slightly more time airborne every day, but I was not timing him. My need to believe that this silly exercise was working undoubtedly outweighed any temporal sense.

We took Paladin from the pond on January 1. On the tenth of January I went over in the morning to exercise Spot and he was gone. There was no carcass, no blood anywhere on the ice or in the surrounding woods—I know, I searched diligently. I stood out on the ice and called "Spot," thinking he might be practicing on his own. No goose. I went home and reported what my heart wanted to hear, that Spot was flying just fine and had gone off to a better place to winter.

That was years ago, and I do not see Spot anymore. I hope that he is off living the life of the goose somewhere nearby. However, wondering what became of Spot is not what occupies my mind in the retelling of this story. Even though I am trying to construct this story as Spot's, it is not the line of his *life* that I wish to present as the narrative line. I am more interested in presenting, at greater risk, the tale created by his *choice*, by his individual action. What made Spot stay on the pond in winter with a goose who was failing to thrive and an injured female mallard duck? It is my contention that this is a question we *may* ask—conferring on birds, on all animals, that sense of mind that responds, minutely and individually, to the ebb and flow of life. That we cannot *answer* the question does not disprove the presence of animal mindfulness. What are we to make of Spot's enterprise?

What we know about geese caring for other geese, what we know about geese acting in the best interests of self-preservation, does not explain Spot's actions, but rather throws them into sharper relief. What we need is the story. The short version of the story of Spot is that he stayed on the pond in winter with another goose, who was sick, and an injured duck. He had been in the company of both of these birds earlier in his life, during the later summer and fall on the pond. Spot was not a mother goose, not even—and here you have to trust my reckoning of goose age by size and social skills—old enough to have had any parenting skills. His staying on the pond did not materially affect the chances of either of his two companions' surviving. I do not know that he ever chased off a predator. Although an angry goose is threatening, I doubt even an angry Spot—wings outstretched, neck extended, full honking and hissing mode—could have prevented a hungry fox or coyote from getting at Alcott or Paladin.

He stayed on the frozen pond even though he *knew* that he could fly away. Because when he flew over my head he was not startled into flight, he simply took off. Call it instinct—but what instinct are we to call it? Or call it choice. That is the more provocative option. Spot stayed on the pond in winter with the dying goose and the disabled duck as their companion. He was there for them, and when they didn't need him anymore, he took himself off to safety and a more normal goose life. Leaving me dumbfounded, standing in the cold, in the middle of an icebound pond in the short days and long nights of January. In the isolation of the human mind, looking for reasons.

The minds of the birds, the lives of the birds, are not accessible through the workings of the human mind alone. We must be willing to take the testimony of animal lives as life's own vindication. Receiving the testimony of individual animal lives does mean spending time with them, in the places they live, in all seasons and times and weather—getting cold and wet and learning to walk on ice and to suffer loss. It also means becoming more aware of the movements of mind that chatter and clatter and interfere with our reception of the testimony of animals. I am sure I have not removed the chatter and clatter herein. I have tried to identify it as such and to identify that within me which has responded to the testimony of the animals whose stories I am telling: sg, Mom and Dad, all the goslings, Paladin, and Spot. If I can do this, perhaps I will rediscover kindness, the kinship that I have with all of nature.

I have been to quite a few presentations in the last few years where scientists measure and define and forecast, in an effort to determine what rational state of mind we need to assume to come up with a reasonable way to preserve what we have decided is "nature." These people, for all their good intentions, are not listening to the testimony of the natural world. We cannot justify the ways of trees and birds with numbers; we cannot understand, categorize, describe, value, or predict even the actions of one Canada goose on a rural New England pond in winter.

Walking around the pond from day to day, month after month—watching the snapping turtle lay her eggs and the geese rear their young—the enclosures of my human life had been opened. I had become more susceptible to the kindnesses of birds. After all, it was a bird who had set me off along this path. When sg stood up before me and let me follow him, he took me back into a kinship we have almost forgotten. When Spot exercised his prerogative for compassion by staying on the pond in winter, it was not only Alcott and Paladin who benefited from his grace. By his grace I realized that my motivation to save the injured birds on the ice might be something other than noblesse oblige, something not anthropocentric at all. I was simply reacting to my fellow animals with the same heart that beats in a goose.

To Hear Him Again

Life is everywhere. When we think of life as something granted to us, we forget to look at it closely. The bubbles in ice, the nutrients in grass, the fitness of a feather for flight are all life swirling along. Sunlight in October is life waiting to be deciphered, and birds know the code. Life is more than chemistry, biology, physics. Becoming and being require care, patience, courage, desire, and fear—and accepting loss. And some other mysterious quality we cannot name for certain.

I set out to know how SG lived in order to save his life. Along the way I thought I could tell his story. When I realized how much I would have to see and taste, to feel and experience in order to tell the story of one goose, and then the stories of the adventures he led me to, I knew that I could not tell the whole story. So I chose to put together this book for SG, this collection of the pieces of the days through which I followed him. I give this collection back to him, out of admiration for the respect he has shown for life, in gratitude for what he has led me to see, and out of a deep affection nurtured by the time we spent together.

On the walk over to the pond I watched the passing of light and warmth express itself in the milkweed pods' formation and efflu-ence. Black-eyed Susans were gaudy along every fence line, until insects and frost spent their gold. Mushrooms came—bright reds and milky whites, the yellow chanterelles and the occasional purple, the fluorescent orange slimes and jellies—and went. They are only the small, short-lived blossoms of enormous underground communities. Deferential, I walked over this vital family all day. I walked past the places where the turtleheads bloom in late summer, where the nodding bur marigold marks the line between water and land in early autumn. All of this pleasure taken in ritual, all of this joyful familiarity, all of the sweet sensuality of naming is mine because a solitary goose brought me to the pond and the woods every day.

Geese tend to return to the same place to raise their young, year after year, so in the early spring of 1999 I was haunting the pond looking for Mom and Dad. They were there in late March, so I looked forward to a spring of goslings. At the same time, I realized it had been several months since I had visited SG at Hungerford. One sunny afternoon in April—one of those days of soft, daffodil-colored light—I drove the now-familiar route to New Britain. None of the regular staff were there, and the staff who were there were busy with a group of children. However, they waved me through when I introduced myself (I think I had attained benefactress status) and I went through the doors into the yard. No geese except the very disabled. My chest went hollow. Yet, I could hear geese. I had heard Joe refer to a small pond just outside the fence where he sometimes took the geese for a few hours on a nice afternoon. I found my way down there and sure enough, there were geese. But none of them were SG. It had been months, but he could not have changed appearance that radically. None of these geese had his long neck. None of them had white markings so high behind the eyes. None of these geese responded to my voice. I turned away from their lovely interlude and went back to the main house, where I left a note for Joe to call me. I had the entire hour of my drive

back to go through the scenarios: sg had died of some lung infec-
tion (common in flightless birds); sg had gotten caught by a fox or
coyote who had gotten over the fence (it wasn't really much of a
fence); sg had become antisocial and had had to be put down. All
of my scenarios were to explain sg's death.

Joe called within two days, apologizing for not having called
me sooner. I sat down and steeled myself for the words I expected.
I was glad for the exercised control, because the words were not
what I expected. sg had regained his ability to fly—unheard of
after two years on the ground. Joe had found him trying out a short
liftoff one day and had arranged for him to go to a rehabilitator in
March. That was the reason for the apology; he felt he should have
called me then. He gave me the name of the rehabilitator.

The rehabilitator did not know me and, undoubtedly, could not
understand any of the urgency in the voice on her answering ma-
chine. It was the busy season, when young birds are injured or
abandoned or orphaned, so she did not call for two weeks after my
initial message. Oh, yes, she had taken two geese from Hungerford
earlier in the year and, having watched them and checked them
out, put them on a pond where they would be safe. They had both
taken off with a flock that came by. She'd seen them come and go
since then. Yes, one was banded, and he was still with the flock.
No, she couldn't give me directions to the pond; it was on private
property. Good-bye.

So that was it. A success. sg was a three-year-old gander; maybe
he would even meet a nice goose and settle down to raise goslings.
If he did, he would probably settle near her home territory; that
was the way it usually worked. He probably would not find his way
back to Bicentennial (although I would look for him for years). I
would most likely never see him again. Yet, what could be better
than flying free, in the world on the other side of the glass?

Notes

Epigraph

Du Fu, "Lone Wild Goose," in *The Selected Poems of Du Fu*, trans. Burton Watson (New York: Columbia University Press, 2002), 148.

Two Solitary Figures

1. Marcel Gil Minnaert, *The Nature of Light and Colour in the Open Air* (Mineola, N.Y.: Dover, 1954).

2. Paula Gunn Allen, ed., *Spider Woman's Granddaughters: Traditional Tales and Contemporary Writing by Native American Women* (Boston: Beacon Press, 1989).

3. Jean-Jacques Rousseau, *Meditations of a Solitary Walker*, trans. Peter France (New York: Penguin Books, 1995).

Footprints

1. Konrad Z. Lorenz, *King Solomon's Ring: New Light on Animal Ways*, trans. Marjorie Kerr Wilson (1952; reprint, Alexandria, Va.: Time-Life Books, 1962), xxiv–xxv. Citations are to the 1962 edition.

2. Elizabeth Marshall Thomas, *The Hidden Life of Dogs* (1993; reprint, New York: Simon & Schuster, 1995), 3–4. Citations are to the 1995 edition.

3. Mary Austin, *The Land of Little Rain* (1903; reprint, New York: Penguin Books, 1988), 10. Citations are to the 1988 edition.

4. Ibid., 11.

5. Jeffrey Moussaieff Masson and Susan McCarthy, *When Elephants*

Weep: The Emotional Lives of Animals (1995; reprint, New York: Dell, 1996), xxi–xxii. Citations are to the 1996 edition.

6. Austin, *Land*, 12.

7. Tom Regan, *The Case for Animal Rights* (Berkeley: University of California Press, 1983). The discussion of the subject-of-a-life criterion is central to the chapter "Justice and Equality," on pages 232–65.

8. Thomas, *Hidden Life*, 120.

9. George Schaller, *The Last Panda* (Chicago: University of Chicago Press, 1993), 79–80.

10. Diane Boyd-Heger, "Living with Wolves," in *Intimate Nature: The Bond Between Women and Animals*, ed. Linda Hogan, Deena Metzger, and Brenda Peterson, 90–96 (New York: Ballantine, 1998), 96.

The Life of a Wild Goose

1. Aldo Leopold, *A Sand County Almanac and Sketches Here and There* (1949; reprint, New York: Oxford University Press, 1987), 23. Citations are to the 1987 edition.

2. Malcolm A. Ogilvie, *Wild Geese* (Vermillion, S.D.: Buteo Books, 1978), 91.

3. Joe Van Wormer, *The World of the Canada Goose* (Philadelphia: J. B. Lippincott, 1968), 99–100.

4. Sigurd Olson, "Wild Geese," in *The Bird Watcher's Anthology*, ed. Roger Tory Peterson, 32–35 (New York: Harcourt, Brace, 1957), 33, 35.

5. Pattiann Rogers, "Eulogy for a Hermit Crab," in *Firekeeper: New and Selected Poems* (Minneapolis, Minn.: Milkweed Editions, 1994), 79.

Ice

1. Quotation is from Robert Frost's poem "Desert Places," in *The Poetry of Robert Frost*, ed. Edward Connery Lathem (1969; reprint, New York: Henry Holt, 1979), 296. Citations are to the 1979 edition.

A Bird Who Cannot Fly

1. National Wildlife Rehabilitators Association, *Principles of Wildlife Rehabilitation: The Essential Guide for Novice and Experienced Rehabili-

tators (1997; reprint, St. Cloud, Minn.: National Wildlife Rehabilitators Association, 1998), 3. Citations are to the 1998 edition.

2. Ibid., 17.

3. Laura Simon, letter to author, March 2000.

4. Irene Ruth, speaking at the Connecticut Wildlife Rehabilitators Association Spring Meeting, April 2, 2000.

5. NWRA, *Principles*, 451.

6. Taunya A. Netich, letter to author, March 2000.

7. Irigaray's work is discussed by Eléanor H. Kuykendall in her essay "Toward an Ethic of Nurturance: Luce Irigaray on Mothering and Power," in *Mothering: Essays in Feminist Theory*, ed. Joyce Trebilcot, 264–74 (Totowa, N.J.: Rowman & Allanheld, 1984).

8. Ibid., 264.

9. Jayne Amico, speaking at the Connecticut Wildlife Rehabilitators Association Spring Meeting, April 2, 2000.

10. Linda Hogan, "First People," in *Intimate Nature* (see p. 132, note 10), 15.

11. Marian Scholtmeijer, "The Power of Otherness: Animals in Women's Fiction," in *Animals and Women: Feminist Theoretical Explorations*, ed. Carol J. Adams and Josephine Donovan, 231–62 (Durham, N.C.: Duke University Press, 1995), 233.

Wild Poems

1. Donald Stokes, *A Guide to Bird Behavior*, vol. 1 (Boston: Little, Brown, 1979), 26.

2. Van Wormer, *World*.

3. David Goodnow, *How Birds Fly* (Columbia, Md.: Periwinkle Books, 1992), 12.

4. Chris Elphick, John B. Dunning Jr., and David Allen Sibley, eds., *The Sibley Guide to Bird Life and Behavior* (New York: Alfred A. Knopf, 2001), 29–30.

5. Van Wormer, *World*, 84.

6. Elphick, Dunning, and Sibley, *Sibley Guide*, 18–20.

7. Information available from the Coalition to Prevent the Destruction of Canada Geese, www.canadageese.org.

8. Ogilvie, *Wild Geese*, 292.

Geese, Geese, Geese, Geese, Geese

1. Edwin Way Teale, ed., *Audubon's Wildlife* (New York: Viking 1964), 137.

2. Harold C. Hanson, *The Giant Canada Goose* (Carbondale: Southern Illinois University Press, 1965).

3. See www.birds.cornell.edu.

4. Jerome B. Robinson, "Return of the Home-Grown Honker," *Field and Stream* (Northeast edition) 102, no. 27 (1997): 8.

5. William K. Stevens, "Migrant Geese Face Cloudy Future," *New York Times*, September 10, 1996, sec. 3.

6. Howard Norman, *The Girl Who Dreamed Only Geese and Other Tales of the Far North* (New York: Harcourt, Brace, 1997), 129.

7. Ibid., 140–41.

8. Richard Roberts, "Born to Be Wild," *Wildlife Conservation* 99 (Sept./Oct. 1996): 34.

9. Hope Ryden, *God's Dog: A Celebration of the North American Coyote* (New York: Lyons & Burford, 1989).

10. Diana Muir, "Where the Wild Things Are: NYC," *Boston Globe*, July 22, 2001, Books, D4.

The End of Gazing

1. John Berger, "Why Look at Animals?" in *About Looking* (New York: Pantheon Books, 1980), 5.

2. Ibid., 13.

3. Berger, "Why Look," 2.

4. John Tallmadge, "Toward a Natural History of Reading," in *Interdisciplinary Studies in Literature and Environment* 7, no. 1 (2000): 33–45.

5. Barbara Noske, *Humans and Other Animals: Beyond the Boundaries of Anthropology* (London: Pluto Press, 1989), 62–63.

6. Susanne Kappeler, "Speciesism, Racism, Nationalism . . . or the Power of Scientific Subjectivity," in *Animals and Women* (see chapter 6, note 11), 320–52.

7. Jim Papa, "Death on the Wing," in *Interdisciplinary Studies in Literature and Environment* 6, no. 1 (1999): 111.

8. Rachel Carson, *Under the Sea Wind* (1941; reprint, New York: Dutton, 1991), 65, 68. Citations are to 1991 edition.

9. Berger, "Why Look."

10. Hogan, "First People," 15.

11. Noske, *Humans and Other Animals*, 120–60.

12. Linda Vance, "Beyond Just-So-Stories: Narrative, Animals, and Ethics," in *Animals and Women* (see chapter 6, note 11), 185.